Alexander Hamilton Vinton

Four Lectures Delivered in the Church of the Holy Trinity

Second Edition

Alexander Hamilton Vinton

Four Lectures Delivered in the Church of the Holy Trinity
Second Edition

ISBN/EAN: 9783337290009

Printed in Europe, USA, Canada, Australia, Japan

Cover: Foto ©Lupo / pixelio.de

More available books at **www.hansebooks.com**

BOHLEN LECTURES, INAUGURAL SERIES.

FOUR LECTURES

Delivered in the Church of the Holy Trinity, Philadelphia, in the Year 1877,

ON THE

FOUNDATION OF THE LATE JOHN BOHLEN, Esq.

BY

ALEXANDER H. VINTON, D.D.

SECOND EDITION.

NEW YORK:
THOMAS WHITTAKER,
2 and 3 Bible House,
1887.

Printed for the Rector, Churchwardens, and Vestrymen of the Church of the Holy Trinity, Philadelphia, Trustees of the John Bohlen Lectureship.

THE JOHN BOHLEN LECTURESHIP.

JOHN BOHLEN, who died in this city on the twenty-sixth day of April, 1874, bequeathed to trustees a fund of $100,000, to be distributed to religious and charitable objects in accordance with the well-known wishes of the testator.

By a deed of trust, executed June 2, 1875, the trustees under the will of Mr. Bohlen transferred and paid over to "The Rector, Church-wardens, and Vestrymen of the Church of the Holy Trinity, Philadelphia," in trust, a sum of money for certain designated purposes, out of which fund the sum of $10,000 was set apart for the endowment of THE JOHN BOHLEN LECTURESHIP, upon the following terms and conditions:—

"The money shall be invested in good, substantial, and safe securities, and held in trust for a fund to be called 'The John Bohlen Lectureship,' and the income shall be applied annually to the payment of a qualified person, whether clergyman or layman, for the delivery and publication of at least one hundred copies of two or more lecture sermons. These lectures shall be delivered at such time and place, in the city of Philadelphia, as the persons nominated to appoint the lecturer shall from time to time determine, giving at least six months' notice to the person appointed to deliver the same, when the same may conveniently be done, and in no case selecting the same person as lecturer a second time within a period of five years. The payment shall be made to said lecturer, after the lectures have been printed and received by the trustees, of all the income for the year derived from said fund, after defraying the expense of printing the lectures and the other incidental expenses attending the same.

"The subject of such lectures shall be such as is within the terms set forth in the will of the Rev. John Bampton for the delivery of what are known as the 'Bampton Lectures,' at Oxford, or any other subject distinctively connected with or relating to the Christian religion.

"The lecturer shall be appointed annually in the month of May, or as soon thereafter as can conveniently be done, by the persons who for the time being shall hold the offices of Bishop of the Protestant Episcopal Church of the Diocese in which is the Church of the Holy Trinity; the Rector of said church; the Professor of Biblical Learning, the Professor of Systematic Divinity, and the Professor of Ecclesiastical History, in the Divinity School of the Protestant Episcopal Church in Philadelphia.

"In case either of said offices are vacant, the others may nominate the lecturer."

Under this trust the Rev. ALEXANDER H. VINTON, D.D., of Boston, was appointed to deliver the lectures for the year 1877.

PHILADELPHIA, Easter, 1877.

LECTURE I.

THE PERSONALITY OF GOD.

CONTENTS.

LECTURE I.
THE PERSONALITY OF GOD 9

LECTURE II.
THE TRI-PERSONALITY OF GOD. 39

LECTURE III.
THE ATONEMENT 73

LECTURE IV.
THE HOLY GHOST 105

LECTURE I.

THE PERSONALITY OF GOD.

IN accepting the invitation to inaugurate this series of the Bohlen Lectures, I enjoyed a peculiar pleasure, a pleasure tinged with the sweetness of a certain sadness.

The title is a memorial of him with whom I was once connected by official ties, for whom I cherished an affectionate personal regard, and whose character I held in most respectful esteem. I remembered the kindness of his temper, the readiness of his heart, the fixedness of his conscience, his unfailing labors of beneficence; in a word, I remembered the supremacy of the piety that suggested his motives, controlled his life, shaped his character, and inspired him with such loving consecration of self to his Saviour and

Lord as branched out spontaneously and gladly into all good words and works. His religion was his life, whose sovereign impulse, the glory of Christ, directed itself into all the channels of beneficence and subsidized his culture and his wealth for the good of his fellow-men. It was in perfect keeping with his character, therefore, that his dying wish should be for the holy faith which he had loved and lived for and had taught for many years to successive classes of young men; that his teaching might survive in other utterances than his, and still be his; that in a larger way and with a certain perpetuity he might still speak, though dead. Hence the institution of this lectureship, his apt memorial,—better than wreathed flowers cast upon his coffin and smothered in his grave: living plants, rather, whose fresh fragrance is restored as the seasons return; better than marble effigy, coldly glittering in its solitariness; a memorial, rather, that lives and speaks to passing men, and speaks, as he himself would speak, of the great salvation. So may these lectures always speak, just as he would have them do, of the truth as it is in Jesus!

To this loving recognition, which my heart could not refuse, of my former associate and friend, may I not add a word, congratulating myself that I stand once more before you, the congregation to whom fifteen years ago I ministered in the things of the gospel? I do so with the more assurance because I know that whatever of superseding influences may have come between your hearts and me in that long interval, yet the occasion and the name it bears will at least gain for me a welcome.

In suggesting this course of lectures, our friend left ample range in the choice of topics. They might be gathered from the whole fertile field of theology, and grouped at the discretion of the lecturer. As I scanned this field, it was plain that among its crowd of theories there were some subsidiary doctrines, which had once been interesting, but had lost their freshness with the exigency that begat them.

There were other topics, however, whose importance is as rich and constant as the relation between God and the soul, that are now encountering the antagonism of our sceptical and aggressive age. Of these truths I have made choice of four to be the subjects of as many lectures. The first, "The Personality of God"; the second, "His Triune Subsistence"; the third, "His Redemptive Work for Man, the Atonement of Christ"; and the fourth, "His Curative and Sanctifying Agency in Man, the Power and Work of the Holy Ghost." Whenever unbelief would make its fiercest onslaught upon the faith of Christians, it aims at the first of these truths; and whenever the spirit of error in the church becomes pronounced, it has always selected one or another or all of the other three.

These four truths embody themselves in the most prominent statements of our creed, and in treating them I will make those statements my starting-points.

In discussing, therefore, the first of these topics, the personality of God, I denote its import in these words: "I believe in one God, the Father Almighty, Maker of heaven and earth, and of all things visible and invisible." This general statement involves these derivative statements, viz.: The universe has a personal Creator, whose nature and attributes are infinite, and in virtue of that personality he is capable of coming into personal relations with us, so that he can be to us a Father and we can be to him as children.

Ever since men began to think, they have thought about God, that is, they have thought about the origin of the world, and how anything came to exist. The Oriental philosophies, older, perhaps, by thousands of years than our Christianity, busied themselves with this chief thought, and so did the schools of the Grecian philosophy. The cosmogony, the theory of the universe, was the one burden of their speculations. In the Middle Ages philosophy dealt more with ideas that lie this side of those primary ones. Assuming the existence of God, they discussed his counsels and his plans, and his relations to mankind, and might rather be called theologies. At a still more recent date there started up again a philosophy that engrossed almost the whole of German thought. It was a speculative system throughout. It began its thinking outside of the visible world, and its reasoning, drawn from *à priori* assumptions, was directed not so much to show what is the constitution of the universe as to prove what it must be. This, which was called the spiritual philosophy, was by a return of the pendulum of thought replaced by the materialistic system of our day, which confines itself to the investigation of the structure and forces of the world about us.

With this system we have been made sufficiently familiar from the presence among us of Huxley and Tyndall and Proctor as its spokesmen and apostles, and from the writings that occupy the counters of the book-stores, the pages of the reviews, the columns of the newspapers. It forms the staple of our common talk in the parlors and the railroad-cars, so that not to know something of this system is to betray the lack of finished culture.

The whole long category of philosophical systems, comprehending all the great and various thinking of the world, may be resolved into two systems, one of them pantheism and the other materialism,—pantheism beginning with the abstract and the possible and reasoning forward to explain the actual; and the other beginning with the actual and tracing it back towards the abstract

The Personality of God. 15

and the invisible, but stopping short at both. If men think at all on philosophical themes they must think from one or the other of these two standing-points, so that there can be but two essential philosophies. Moreover, among the whole long list of philosophical thinkers from seven hundred years before Christ down to the present hour, almost none have been led by their thinking to recognize a personal God. Among the ancients Anaxagoras was the first to maintain that the universe was governed by a personal mind; yet he made but little use of the idea in his system and he had no important following.

There was no school of believers in a personal Deity. Hippocrates, the father of medicine, did indeed so far accept the opinion as to maintain that the Deity might be invoked to help the good effect of his prescriptions. Besides this I know of no other instance in which the pagan philosophy came near touching with one of its fingers the revealed truth of a personal and parental God. The two great philosophies were essentially atheistic.

The system of pantheism is most clearly expounded by Spinoza, its modern reviver. Spinoza held that there was one eternal something which he called "substance." He did not mean material substance, nor perhaps anything that we call spiritual, but it was an existence of some sort, without intelligence and without voluntary powers or any attributes that could betoken personality.

It was the nature of this eternal substance to radiate and evolve itself continually, and in doing so it took on visible and tangible shapes and effloresced into a material universe. This universe, passing on through the stages of life and decay, was resolved back again to its original matrix to be again evolved and decay, and so to chase its own life round and round in a never-ending circuit.

Thus the visible world was only the necessary form of this eternal substance, spinning itself out from itself and winding itself back into itself. If we call that eternal substance God, then God was the world itself, and the world itself was God.

Now Spinoza did call this substance God, and since he made that substance to be the all in all of everything, his contemporaries called him a "God-intoxicated man."

This is essential pantheism according to its ablest

The Personality of God.

expositor. We see that it must be godless from its want of personality. We can hold no communion with that eternal substance, because it is unintelligent ; we cannot supplicate nor deprecate it, for it has no feeling and no will ; we cannot worship it, for it has no character. There can be no moral distinction, no right, no wrong, because everything that happens is but the evolution of God.

As it has no connection with us but in material forms, so our nearest approach to it is in the admiration of nature and in the indulgence of our natural desires. I said just now that so much of the philosophy as has ever been in the world that was not pantheistic was materialistic, and this, like the other, denied the personality of God. Almost all the earlier philosophers were of this school, and ever since then the fashion of thinking has vibrated between pantheism and materialism, and each has held an alternate and royal sway in the realm of philosophy.

Materialism teaches that the world is made up of two principles of matter and motion, and that when the action of motion upon matter is begun, matter is evolved, by necessary laws of its being, into a universe of varied forms and lives.

The old materialism did not differ from the modern in these fundamental principles. Its philosophy was the same, although it was far less rich in its knowledge of the facts of Nature and of the affinities that work out her changes. In this knowledge our modern materialistic science is affluent beyond all precedent. I remind you only of a truism when I say that the rise of our modern science has been like a dayspring to the intellectual and physical life of our century. At her word of command our civilization has sprung forward, at a single bound, farther than in many weary generations of the ages gone. By developing and utilizing the forces of nature, she has rendered labor and its products so facile and sure that in convenience, comfort, and physical enjoyment life seems to be concentrated to a focus ; and the processes by which her achievements have been won are some of them amazing feats of intellectual vigor. The nebular hypothesis of the formation of the world, that glorious guess of Laplace, reaching into the realms of conjecture, and bringing back its far-off conceptions, verified by all the known phenomena of the universe, has almost a supernatural look. The suggestion of an imponderable ether surrounding and penetrating the fabric of the world—a suggestion outside of experiment, yet explaining the theory of light and perhaps of sound more satisfactorily than any former endeavor—is another of the brilliant, prophetic flashes of scientific thought that almost urge the common mind to cry, " What is man ? Thou hast made him a little, only a little, lower than the angels ! "

Yet these discoveries, being the fruits of hypothesis and not of strict analysis, may be regarded as happy strokes of mental ingenuity rather than as legitimate products of science; for it is the singular quality and boast of modern science that it is purely inductive. Its processes consist in observing and analyzing particular phenomena, arranging them according to their essential likenesses, until the whole of the material world is resolved into its elementary forms. In this, the legitimate sphere of Science, her processes of generalization have developed admirable results. She has assorted all the facts and forces of matter into groups, and learned the laws by which the primal forms of things are organized into a Kosmos, a whole, harmonious world; she has demonstrated that all the forms of matter are only one matter, that the universal variety of things sprang from one primordial germ: but her chief and happiest generalization has been in resolving the various material forces into one primal force, of which the rest, are, by a high probability, simply derivations or modifications. These derived forces are therefore congeners,—a sisterhood with one mother, so joined in functions that any one of them may replace and do the work of either of the others.

Although the experiments have not yet been full enough to demonstrate this fact in its entire breadth, yet enough is known to supply a foundation of what is called "the doctrine of the correlation of forces."

That doctrine is described by Prof. Grove, one of its earliest expounders, in these words: "The various affections of matter which constitute the main objects of experimental physics, viz., heat, light, electricity, magnetism, chemical affinity, and motion, are all correlative or have a reciprocal dependence, so that neither, taken abstractedly, can be said to be the essential cause of the others, but either may produce or be convertible into any of the others. Thus heat may mediately or immediately produce electricity, electricity may produce heat, and so of the rest, each merging itself as the force it produces becomes developed; and the same must hold good of the other forces."

The parent force of this united family of forces would seem, in the opinion of Prof. Grove, to be the principle or power of motion; and so the conclusion is that even as the forms of matter are resolvable into one homogeneous matter, so the forces of the world are reducible to one unit of force. Science has taught us, moreover, that this many-sided force operates in all its modifications by fixed and ascertainable methods, which she calls the laws of the material world.

This theory seems, indeed, to encounter among the phenomena of the world at least one exception which refuses to enter into this category of the forces. There is another force, unique in character, which stands outside, as a stranger to the family, if not indeed an antagonist. It is the vital force, the principle of organic life throughout the world, pervading every organism and maintaining each individual existence. It has been attempted, but in the opinion of some scientific men hitherto unsuccessfully, to bring the vital force into correlation with the rest.

There are obvious conditions in which the relationship fails, or if there be relationship it is not that of equality, but rather that of the mastership of the vital force; for it has a sort of formative power that in its normal state controls the working of the other forces, and utilizes them for its own purposes, even neutralizing the action, if need be, of heat and elasticity and chemical affinity, so that itself shall be supreme, as it is singular, in every organism. And when once the vital force has become extinct, it gets no restoring or supplementing help from the rest, but rather they seize upon the lifeless form and rush it into speedy decay, until the once vitalized structure is dissolved into its atoms, which can never be reorganized until the banished force shall come again from its unascertained home and pronounce the vitalizing word "Live!" Yet, notwithstanding the exceptional character of the vital force, the theory of the correlation of forces stands out as a masterly demonstration, and all that is necessary for the purpose to which I would apply it.

There is a wondrous satisfaction to the mind, looking at the complicated machinery of the material world and the promiscuous movements of its seemingly discordant forces, to learn that the discord is truly the most beautiful order, and the promiscuous methods the working of a perfect unity of plan.

These two demonstrations constitute the main theoretic results of modern science. They might seem at first view to be but insignificant results of all the searching thought and labor they have cost; but they are elementary facts of the material world, and, like other elementary things, they contain the possibilities of all things.

Science, therefore, erects her imposing figure before the age, and holds in her lifted hands these two demonstrations as her vouchers of authority. If this were all she did, not one of us would do aught but bow down his mind and do her reverence; but in the pride of her great prowess, she has sometimes advanced the claim that in explaining the system of the material world she has disclosed the whole truth of the universe, and has declared that there is no knowledge besides that which comes from induction, and so Science is understood to be at war with that whole class of conceptions that lie outside of the material world and which are necessarily included in every form of religion. This is the reason why science and religion are nowadays understood to be in antagonism to one another, specially in the fundamental idea of a personal God. I would like to show that so far is this from being true, the actual and admitted results of scientific research are true indicators of a personal Deity. As an inductive system, science ought not to be reproached for not recognizing a Deity in the world. This is not one of the demonstrations that belong to induction. Induction is pure observation, and all the faculties required in an inductive process are the perceptive faculties, and God is not an object of perception.

It were as great an error for Science to undertake to demonstrate a Deity by her processes as it is for her to claim that the perceptive faculties are the only ones we have for the discovery of truth, while these faculties really belong to the lowest tier of man's mental endowments.

Above the level of the perceptions there is the realm of reason, which is the birthplace of all our higher powers and conceptions. Our deepest apprehensions of truth, our loftiest motives, our sublimest reach of thought, spring in a region where the perceptive powers have no play and no place. They all come from the intuitions of reason, certain first principles, which are not so much thoughts as they are conditions, without which the mind cannot think at all.

The axioms of mathematics are of this sort,— conceptions of the pure reason not evolved by experiment. The ideas of unity, of cause, of power, of time, space, infinitude, are born of the mind itself. The mind cannot live without them. Science slurs them as metaphysical and worthless, yet Science cannot carry out a demonstration without adopting the terminology of metaphysics. She speaks of cause and effect, which are metaphysical conceptions purely, for science never saw a cause, but only sequence; and of force, yet no one ever analyzed a force; and of unity, which she constantly reaches after but never saw in nature; and of space and time and infinitude, ideas which turn the perceptive faculties into a mockery. Science ought therefore frankly to admit both the reality and the authority of reason as a faculty far outreaching the possibilities of perception, and adapted to explore those higher truths which the perceptive faculties were not made to learn.

When we have been brought to the last conclusions of Science, force guided by unity of method and law, if we should accept her dictum, that we had learned all that can be known of the truth of the universe, we should be indeed left to a total godlessness of mind. But man's nature refuses to be defrauded of its birthright of reason, refuses to have its divine prerogative of thinking ignored by any system which, with all its claims to respect, still denies a thousand times more knowledge than it possesses; and so, when Science brings forth her demonstrations, Reason at once accepts them, and makes them the starting-point for a flight to higher truth.

In this way material Science answers her true character as a guide and janitor, leading the mind gracefully to the doorway of a higher realm, and saying, " I can teach you no more. Enter up now among the sublimities of truth. Farewell!" Reason begins, then, with the scientific fact of the unit of force. And what is force? What is its source and origin? Science has already told us that the several forces of the world are not primitive but derived forces. She tells us that when the billiard player propels the ivory balls about the table, each ball driving the next, the force is not in the ivory. Is it in the wooden cue? Not there. In the bones and muscles of the player's arm? Still not there. These are only the conveyancers of force. Follow up the line of power and you find it springing fresh-born from the will of the player. This is the ultimate conception of the origin of force, the product of volition verified as a fact by our own intimate consciousness. No proof can go behind this. It is as absolute as the consciousness of life itself. The child learns it when, putting forth its little arm, it encounters a resisting thing, and musters an effort to push it aside. The conscious volition and the conception of power come into birth together in the child's mind, and abide together as long as his conscious life. Nature teaches us, then, that force is the essential product of will; and it follows hence that behind the grand unit of force which actuates and pervades the world there abides a mighty will whose volition is the going forth of the universal life. But the question springs up to the causal faculty of reason, What is the character of this mighty will? Is it a blind, impulsive force, rushing forth in contortions and spasms of effort, without aim or purpose? Science answers this question for us in advance, for she discloses throughout the universe a single great law or method by which all the forces of the world are guided to their destinations. Various as those methods seem, they act all in perfect harmony, and are all reducible back to a unit of law co-ordinate with the unit of force. And this harmony is not the work of chance. Chance is an alien in the realm of science. Science shuts her doors against the crazy intruder. Order, arrangement, plan, whatsoever requires to be developed by mind, must itself be the product of mind. Whatsoever comes into the intelligence must have sprung from intelligence. To make an intelligible product there must be an intelligent producer. The great will, then, is not blind nor wild nor fatalistic. It is a clear-eyed and wise will, giving out a force that moves always by rule and destination. If the universal force is the outcome of will, so the universal order is the expression of intelligence. And now let us remember that both intelligence and will are the distinctive attributes of personality. We can think of them in no other than a personal relation. If this be so, we have been guided by the teachings of Science herself to the magnificent conclusion of a personal being, super-material in his nature, endowed with the intelligence and power that upholds the universe. Thus we have reached a firm stand-point for fresh exploration. Does this wise force comprehend all that belongs to the sovereign of creation ? Let Nature respond once more: Thus far we have inquired only among the laws of the insensible world. Let us try the ascending scale of creation, and here at the top we behold the human creature, man. He sits as a king, endowed, like the Creator himself, with intelligence and will, as if he were not merely a product but rather a portrait of the great Creator; not only demonstrating but illustrating him,—a sort of type of that grand personality to which science has introduced us, as the archetype. In this new subject of observation we discover a property we did not discover in the material world. We find in man a moral element which is in truth the surpassing dignity of his nature, unique as it is lofty.

The material world could not teach us of this, for matter has no moral sense. As we see it in man it seems to sit on his soul as on a throne, the imperial faculty of his nature. True, it is imperfect, with spots upon its face and with its power broken by many a hard strain, but the ideal character of man's moral nature is glorious. Its conceptions mount up to perfection, its regal voice has the power of thunder; and yet it is remarkable that, grand as it is, it always recognizes a moral sovereignty above itself, to which it bows down, of which it stands in awe. If man is by nature a moral being, and if the Creator cannot be inferior to his own work, then the Creator, too, is a moral being. The intuition of reason, the causative faculty, grasps this fresh discovery, and transfers the conception from the typical creature to the archetypal Creator, and then the presence stands before us in its completeness. Look at it, then, as nature and reason have revealed him,—a supernatural personage, mighty, wise, and good, worthy to be God. Induction has guided us to the limits of her demonstrations, the intuitive reason has led those demonstrations to the point of assurance. But, still with this assurance of the personal Creator, a question arises, How great is he? Is he great enough to be the finality of my peace and joy?

In other words, although we have found a being with power enough to create the world, with wisdom enough to order it, and with enough of moral goodness to govern it justly and kindly, yet how far do these qualities reach? I may be satisfied to say with the creed, "I believe in the Creator of heaven and earth"; but can I believe that his power is unlimited so that I can say, "Almighty"? I may say I believe in God, but can I say that his moral goodness is without possible deduction, so that I can call him the only God? And Reason answers her own question. Her intuitions disclose the transcendental truths of time and space and infinitude and unity as the properties of existence, and as soon as the intuition of causality has revealed the personal first cause, the other intuitions combine to clothe the conception with the necessary attributes of infinity. The first cause must be eternal. If his is a necessary existence he must exist alone, since there cannot be two necessary existences; and for the same reason he must exist everywhere; and since his attributes must be as necessary as his existence, they, too, must be infinite, his power absolute, his knowledge taking in the past, the present, and the possible, his moral goodness utterly perfect. But some may say, "How does reason teach us all this of the Creator, since reason cannot conceive of infinitude in any form?" If it is meant that we cannot comprehend the infinite as to its modes, it is most true; but if it means that we cannot conceive of it as a fact, it is most fallacious, for it is impossible to conceive of the opposite. We cannot conceive of space and duration as necessarily limited. Assign any boundary you please, count the miles by millions, billions, and trillions, at each step, and count for years, and when you reach the boundary, and look out beyond, what do you see? Either space or nothing, infinite space or infinite nothing, but still the infinite. And so with duration as with space. Reason will admit of no terminus. She conceives of the infinite and goes out after it forever. Her home is infinitude, and when she finds her God and shows him to us, He is the embodiment of it; He is clothed with it as with a garment, and all his attributes are only different expressions of infinitude. So far then our best-taught reason accepts the creed of God almighty, maker of all things visible and invisible,—accepts this creed so completely that if we admit a personal deity at all we cannot conceive of him as anything less than infinite. But the Christian creed has added another title,—" Father." Do the conclusions we have reached justify the addition? I think so.

If God is indeed the moral archetype of his creature man, a moral personality with infinitude added, then every moral and affectionate perfection may be affirmed of him. If he is infinitely righteous, he will not be unjust to his moral creature; if he is good in the same measure, he will do whatsoever is kind and gracious, strong to help man's weakness, wise to correct and remedy his foolishness, kind and compassionate, not only to relieve his wants, but to forecast the human need, both of body and soul, and to establish a providence that shall run parallel with both. In a word, the idea of the divine fatherhood acknowledges a revelation to man as a necessary outcome of his justice and his goodness. It admits the perfect reasonableness of miracles; it enforces the power and worth of prayer. All the needs of the conscience, the heart, the soul of man are so many specific conclusions that God's fatherhood will prove itself true. In contemplating these needs we get a better view of that fatherhood than we could in the clear, cool heights where our thoughts have been just now ranging.

Our souls grasp it more closely when we bring it down from that high light which is the life of reason, and let it in among the murky things of life, to walk with us over the uneven earth, and enter our homes, where there are cares and trials and fears and sorrows. For the soul must have her creed. Our reason may rejoice to claim the personality of God as a demonstrated truth, but the soul craves the fatherhood; she is not satisfied to say, I believe in an Almighty Creator of heaven and earth. She marks the missing title, "Father," and she asks with anguish, Is there no love, no care, no nurture with the Almighty for his children?

If this big question of the soul were not met to the full, what a grim chimera would our life be, what a palace of ice the demonstration of a God!

The soul can answer her own longings by interpreting her own consciousness.

If I am in his image he will not reject me. He has given me a longing after a perfect bliss that is nowhere else but with him. He teaches me by my earthly loves that there must be infinite loveliness in my God. Nay, the scientific law of adaptation beautifully foreshows that the affinity of the human with the Divine, will be a domestic one, the harmony of heaven and earth, a perfect union. In this let the soul rest, interpreting God by itself.

When the sense of sonship aspires after God, it is because the fatherhood is bending down to lift the soul to itself. When the soul glows with love and trust it is the reflex of the Father's tenderness beaming down upon it.

So God's Fatherhood comes into the life of man, walks with him, talks with him, shines into his darkness, tempers his heats, warms his coldness, and shields him with his right arm, gives peace to die with, triumph over the grave, and an open heaven where reason, soul, and conscience shall see the personal God, and say, Abba Father, I am satisfied. Man's destiny blooms into bliss from this root of faith,—I believe in God the Father Almighty, Maker of heaven and earth, and of all things visible and invisible.

LECTURE II.

THE TRI-PERSONALITY OF GOD.

LECTURE II.

THE TRI-PERSONALITY OF GOD.

MY subject to-night is "The Doctrine of the Trinity." I well know the effect of such an announcement upon very many ears,—a dry, abstract, metaphysical theme, worn worse than threadbare by the collisions of controversy through all the ages; an unpractical theme besides, and not a power in the spiritual life begetting freshness and fruits. Abstract it is, no doubt, and deep and subtle in its suggestions, for it searches the skies and beholds God. It carries the mysterious look of that half-transparent haze that we sometimes see in the summer firmament, tinged with the mellow glory of the midday sun and suggesting an infinite depth of glory beyond: but we can hardly say it is an unpractical theme; we cannot say so of any truth or point of faith which has concentred to itself, as this has, all the other beliefs of the Christian creed from the first year of grace until now.

Nothing can be more striking than the supremely affectionate tenacity with which the generations of Christians have clung to this great doctrine as a sort of "be all and end all" of the universal faith.

While the many minds of the many men have run into diversity on the other points of belief and some into wide tangents of error, there have been very few who believed in Christianity at all who have broken the tether that held them heart and soul to this magnetic centre of the faith.

I do not mean to say that even this doctrine has not been perverted and even denied. Speculative and rationalizing minds have sometimes so explained it as to explain it away, and once for many years, in the Gothic period of the Roman empire, an antagonistic doctrine did so prevail as to threaten fatally this germ-power of the faith. The invading barbarians, in accepting from their conquered foes their religious faith, received it in the form most nearly level with their mental crudeness, and as it was said, "The church awoke one morning and found itself Arian." But even this could not last. The true kingdom of God, which is always within, was stronger than the kingdom of the world. The indwelling Christ in the hearts of believers was a restorative power that by degrees purged out the malaria from the blood and body of the church, and brought back the vigor of her faith, till her strong reclaim established once more the belief of the Divine Trinity as the cardinal truth of the Christian system. This great defection, therefore does not any more than the smaller ones discredit or qualify the statement that the doctrine of the Trinity has been the uniform holding of the church. They have each and all been local and transient, serving only as occasions to bring out into fresh assertion the primitive truth, which might else have lost its brightness and edge.

It may be interesting, I have thought, to track the history of this doctrine, and to note the causes and manner of its development. Development, I say, not in the scientific sense of evolution, starting from an indifferent atom and becoming transformed into all possible shapes; the development rather of a living thing, a plant in whose seed is the potential life of stalk and foliage and fruit, maturing each in its turn as the months go by, first the blade, then the ear, after that the full corn in the ear.

The development of Divine truth is such as never changes its seminal character, but adapts itself with enlargements to suit the ever-new exigencies in the lives of men and the progress of society. We see this beautifully exhibited in the faith of the early church. There was no logical statement of the doctrine of the Trinity. Those early believers were not used to scientific terms or systematic ideas. Their simple faith rested in the leadership and lordship of Jesus Christ. They had accepted him as the all in all of their soul's life and hope. They had consecrated their whole selves to him, living and dying. Their faith in God was not transferred to, but centred in his Son. God was hypostasized to their minds in the person of the Christ; for in the revelation of the Gospel God had so set forth his Son as the author of their salvation, planted him so in the forefront of the great redeeming work, that when they looked for a redeemer they saw only him; when their forgiven souls would embrace their deliverer, they clasped the knees of Christ; when they dedicated their restored and grateful hearts to him to whom they owed so much, it took the form of loyal love and supreme covenanted allegiance to the personal Jesus. They lived for him, they died in him, and their heavenly hope terminated in an everlasting union with him. Jesus Christ was the author not only, but the finisher of their faith. It was not idolatry, for they knew that God was in Christ, reconciling them to himself; and knowing this, they were jealous of any statement that might invade his dignity or abate the assurance of their own trust and hope.

So pre-eminent was this belief in the divinity of Christ among the early Christians, that the first error that enunciated itself was the denial of his humanity, which was thought to derogate from his divinity, maintaining that the person of Jesus was but a phantasm, a mere form, in which God disguised himself when he came down to save the world. The error was repressed, not so much by speculative reasoning as by the Christian consciousness of the church, the divine common-sense, which having been begotten with the new life of Christ in the soul, worked like an inspiration or an instinct to recognize the truth and to detect in the atmosphere of thought the slightest taint of error upon a theme so vital and absorbing as the divinely human person of their Lord. And this state of things lasted through several generations.

The intellectual strength of the church, such as it was, was mainly engaged in vindicating her truths against the assaults of Jews and Pagans, and during this, the apologetic period of her history, there were few speculations within the church touching the doctrines of the faith. Still, in all this period, although there was small occasion for the church to formulate her doctrines in scientific terms, or to define them with logical accuracy, there was evidence enough of the strength and constancy of her faith in the hymns and liturgies brought down from the earliest periods, and universally used. Hymns and liturgies they were, surcharged with the fragrance of a piety that centred its devoutest worship on the divine personality of Christ. And then again there was the surpassing proof of suffering. If the early church gave sometimes only an equivocal testimony to Christ in the party-colored lives of her members, gathered, as they were, from among the various peoples of the empire, with the crust of heathen habits not yet sloughed off from their crude piety; if they were not all versed in the casuistry of a daily godliness,—they were at least clear and stanch enough in their grand holding of Christ to give up their lives rather than to deny him. The shortcomings in little duties might throw a suspicion upon their reverence for their Lord's precepts, but their endurance unto martyrdom left no question of their surpassing love of his person and their supreme trust in his divine salvation.

Martyrdom, therefore, was the voice of the church's faith in the divinity of Christ. The saintly blood that saturated the arena, and flowed in the gutters of the amphitheatre, was a demonstration of the primitive creed that could have borrowed nothing of clearness or emphasis from any argument. The logic of dying carried not only an assertion of the church's faith, but a proof of its truth and power that gained thousands of converts to the divinity of Christ. But by and by, as the church grew towards a settled and secure condition, the minds of men turned more towards the analysis of the creed. It was then only a simple formula, probably like the Apostles' Creed as we now have it, if it was not indeed the same, containing nothing more than a recital of facts from the narrative of the Bible. Yet each fact was the investment of a truth; each historic statement bore within itself a divine meaning; and the minds of men set themselves to eliminate that meaning, and to formulate it in some scientific statement. Then began the intellectual gladiatorship, which is always stirred by thinking upon deep and high themes. The apologetic period passed into the dogmatic. The faith that had hitherto been a warm instinct, finding its sufficient reinforcement in the spiritual needs of a driven and persecuted church, was now called upon to justify itself at the tribunal of the reasoning powers. The main controversy was touching the divinity of Christ.

The doctrine of the Holy Ghost, his personality and agency, was not as yet impugned; neither was it necessary to defend it as a part of the doctrine of the Trinity. For if it could be established that the person of the Son was coequal and coeternal with the person of the Father, then there would be proved a dual oneness in the Godhead that silenced the speculative objectors to the Trinity. Because if the oneness of the Godhead admits of a plurality of persons, it makes no difference in the reason of things whether that plurality be two or three. When the rational difficulty of any plurality at all is met and answered, the question, " How many does that plurality embrace?" is a question for revelation alone to determine.

The controversy gathered itself, therefore, exclusively about the question of the proper and personal divinity of Christ. It was a warfare of ingenious and subtile reasoning on both sides. The profoundest logic and the keenest metaphysical distinctions were the weapons of this ethereal contest, which assumed four distinct aspects answering to as many distinct opinions touching the nature and person of Christ. The first opinion denied his proper divinity; the second denied his possession of a human soul, and maintained that God took the place of the soul in the person of Christ; the third affirmed that there were two distinct persons in Christ, divine and human; and the fourth mingled the two natures of Christ into one. These four errors were condemned by the church, and each error was answered, as Hooker says, by a single word. The first, which denied that Christ was God, is answered by the word "truly." The second, that denied to Christ a perfect humanity from the absence of a human soul, is met by the word "perfectly." The third, that divided his person into two, by the adverb "indivisibly," and the fourth which confounded the two natures by blending them in one, was answered by another adverb, "distinctly." "Truly," "perfectly," "indivisibly," "distinctly," that is, truly God, perfectly man, of one indivisible personality, and of two distinct natures. These four adverbs denote, therefore, the four aspects of the doctrine which, as the sides of a square, enclose the great truth impregnably. Every assault upon the doctrine must make its approach upon one or another of these four sides, which thus complete the statement of the doctrine and exhaust the several forms of objection. This quadrilateral intrenchment of the truth was accomplished by the four General Councils of the church, each pronouncing upon one or another of the four chief heresies. In those councils the total doctrine of the Trinity, involving the distinct personalities of the Father, the Son, and the Holy Ghost joined together in the substantive unity of the divine nature, was so formulated by precise logical terms, sharp-lined and clear, that the crystalline formation has lost no fraction of its meaning to this day nor a scintilla of its bright truth. Answering the speculations of the best reason of man with the deductions of the most rational logic, it left no careless loop for ingenuity to hang a doubt on.

As we trace the light of this doctrine back through the ages of faith till we come to the period of its first systematic statement, it stands out from the background of revelation, condensing the diffusive truth into one luminous body, the fixed exposition of the mind of God.

Thus far, you will observe, I have not entered into the Scriptural evidence of this great doctrine. The collection of texts would be too long a process for a single lecture. Yet I cannot help asking you to think a little of a single text, which seems to me a sort of focal statement of the doctrine. I refer to the baptismal formula drawn from Christ's last commission to his apostles: "Go ye, teach all nations, baptizing them in the name of the Father and of the Son and of the Holy Ghost."

Remembering the occasion of these words, they bear a very peculiar significance. They were the ministerial charter of authority and the guide-book of ministerial responsibility. What Christ said to his disciples in his parting words must bear a weighty meaning. As baptismal words, they institute the sacrament of initiation into his church. Chiselled on the portico of the Christian temple, their meaning must be the alphabetical truth of his religion. Every man or woman or child must adopt these words as the confession of his faith,— "Father, Son, and Holy Ghost."

Let us see what truth is garnered up into this formula of words. And first examine the formula itself as a simple question of grammatical construction, "In the name of the Father and of the

Son and of the Holy Ghost." Here is a noun in the singular number, the word, "name," and then there are three different titles denoting as many distinct personalities; and the word "name" in the singular is made to comprehend the three several titles as if they were together summed up in that one name. The unit and the triplet are identical in force and value. Now this relation is not changed when we turn the abstraction into a personality; as the comprehensive name which takes in the three titles is the name of God, so the three personalities denoted by the titles are personalities of God, and thus the God of our baptism is a triune Jehovah. But leaving the grammatical sense of the baptismal formula, let us see what light is shed upon our subject by the nature and use of the baptism itself.

Baptism is the form of a covenant between the two parties, God and man, in which each party assumes a distinct responsibility and obligation. On the part of God, it is the obligation of grace and salvation. On the part of man, it is self-consecration and obedience. We may look at it both on its divine and the human side. The interpretation of its divine side is this : all the blessing of the covenant, forgiveness of sin, regeneration of the soul, the indwelling of God, spiritual strength and victory to be crowned in Heaven. These are the pledged gifts of baptism to every faithful receiver. But we ask, "In whose name, on what authority, are these matchless promises made?" In the one name, by the one authority, of the Father and of the Son and of the Holy Ghost. But these gifts are all divine, the bestowment of God alone. It cannot be, then, that either of the covenanting persons is less than divine. The Son cannot be a creature born in time, if he bestows creative and eternal gifts. The Holy Ghost must be more than an influence, a breath, an impersonality, if it can work the most illustrious works of God.

And so I infer that since the covenant is one and the authority one, and since the covenanting powers must be personal, there must be a sense in which the distinct personalities must be joined in one substance of unity. The God of baptism must be triune.

Look now at the human side of the baptismal

sacrament. The believing person is baptized in the one name. To him who bears that name he makes confession of his guilt, proclaims the gratitude of forgiveness. Him he avouches to be henceforward the sovereign of his heart and life; renouncing all other conflicting loves, all repugnant service, all other worship, he dedicates himself to his acceptance.

Lost, but redeemed by Him, guilty, but by Him forgiven, sinful in grain, but now by Him regenerated, he brings his whole rescued nature and lays it on the altar consecrated to the one great baptismal name, and that name Father, Son, and Holy Ghost. And the same importunate question comes round to the human side, Who are Father, Son, and Holy Ghost? Am I to pay a sovereign and equal loyalty to the eternal Father, to a creature, and to a breath, an influence, the shadow of a shade? Is my faith to be distributed among beings of such different make and nature, and my supremest love and adoration divided and degraded? Is this what I mean in my baptism? It were idolatry to do so. If I must render to the three persons a divine consecration, then those three must be alike divine. If I must bow to them alike under one sacred name, there must be a sense in which the three are one, and the God of my baptism is triune. I do not see why the force of this reasoning is not conclusive, and interpreting the baptismal text by its grammatical structure and its religious purpose, it seems to contain in itself the necessary recognition of the doctrine of the Trinity,—three distinct personalities joined with equal power and glory in one essential nature of Godhead.

This is the substance of the doctrine as it was adjusted and set forth by the four General Councils, in refutation of all the opposing theories that had come into birth during two centuries of the church's life. And this declaration seems to have been accepted as a finality and treasured as a priceless legacy by all the Christian generations since. It has entered into the creed of every considerable organization of Christians to this day. The Eastern and the Western churches, and every Protestant church that has embodied its faith in a symbol, have clung to the doctrine as the spinal column of the whole body of Christian belief, upon which depended the value and vigor of every other tenet. In all this lapse of time none of the errors that teased the early church have recovered from the buffet of the four councils, except two, the Arian and the Sabellian theories. These two, being less speculative than the rest, more level to the common apprehension of men, would hold their grasp the longest, and seize the first occasion of religious thinking to cast aside their grave-clothes and come forth in a resurrection form.

The Arian heresy consisted in the absolute denial of the deity of Christ. And although the utmost that Arius ever affirmed was that there was a period when the Son of God was not, yet the sensitive perceptions of the early Christians discerned quickly the falsity and mischief that were disguised in this gentle negation, and immediately rose in conflict. The controversy was virulent and widely spread. The Church was shaken by it. The Arian opinion was so simple that it might easily satisfy the minds of the common and uncultured class, who were inapt and impatient at subtile distinctions of thought, and so rational as to suit that other class, always to be found in cultivated society, whose chief worship is paid to the sovereignty of intellect, who would bring divine truth within the jurisdiction of reason, and summon even the deep things of God to justify themselves at the bar of common-sense. Arianism, therefore, was a formidable power of error, which had to be met and refuted by the gathered authority of the church.

The first General Council, assembled at Nicea in A. D. 325, gave such point-blank denial to the Arian position as to shut it out forever from the citadel of the Catholic faith.

"God of God, light of light, very God of very God, begotten not made, being of one substance with the Father," were words of august authority, that uttered the death-warrant of Arianism within the church.

And although it has reappeared again and again in its own form and in the derived and cognate forms of Semiarianism, Unitarianism, and humanitarianism, it has always been as an assailant from the outside, and has never ventured to claim the sanction of Catholic approval; so that while it may claim among its adherents characters as exalted and lives as pure as that of Arius himself, with beliefs so reverent and trustful as to challenge our highest respect, yet its extreme indulgence of reason has begotten much lower forms of belief, until we can count the steps in the ladder of declension, from the highest form of Arian belief down to the disbelief of any supernatural element in the Bible, a total denial of its inspiration, claiming the religion of the absolute as the ultimate reach of reason and the only true faith for mankind. But besides the Arian error, I mentioned the Sabellian as having survived the period of the councils, and reappearing in modern forms.

The error of Sabellius differed from that of Arius by a whole diameter; for while Arius could not but hold the personality of the Son of God, since he believed him to be a creature, Sabellius, on the other hand, maintained his divinity and denied his distinct personality. He held that God subsisted only in one personality, and that in his relations with man he acted in three distinct lines or functions or methods, and in each of these functions or methods he assumed a distinct and descriptive title. As the supreme administrator of the world he bore the title of Father; whenever he would make manifestations of himself to man he assumed the name of Son; and whenever he would bring his power to bear in the way of efficient agency upon man's life and soul, he was called the Holy Ghost. God the sovereign, enthroned amidst the reserve of his majesty, God the manifester, coming into incarnation, and God the regenerator and sanctifier of the human soul, were only three distinct aspects of the one personality of God. There were others, both before and after Sabellius, who held opinions differing only slightly from his, and of whom, therefore, he is a fair representative. It is easy to see how widely and easily his doctrines would find acceptance in the church. By recognizing the full divinity of the Son and of the Holy Ghost, he satisfied the hearts of that devout multitude whose faith and love had centred on a Saviour God, but whose reasoning powers were untrained in logical distinctions. Their hearts and souls had taught them by a delighted experience of his grace that their Christ was divine, and they had not enough of dialectic skill and acumen to trace out the vicious consequence of denying his separate personality. Yet it requires no long thought to discover the sinister bearing of this view upon the doctrine of Christ's atonement.

It seems plain that if the Son of God be only one aspect of the Father's person, the atonement for human guilt was made by the Father to himself, —an incongruity that carries its own refutation. There could be, then, no atonement in its sense of substitution, or in any sense beyond that of moral suasion or a pure example or a pathetic martyrdom. There could be no high-priestly intercession at the mercy-seat above for the struggling souls of the redemption.

The utmost of the work of Christ would be to tell mankind that he was their Father, who had come down to assure them of his fatherhood, that he loved them like a father, pitied their moral weakness, and would by no means judge them severely if they would try to do as he should tell them. There is not enough in a doctrine like this to meet the wants of a soul profoundly in earnest, looking first at its own low proclivities, and then looking at God in the white splendor of his holiness, a soul possessed by a conscious guiltiness that condemns itself, and insists on being punished.

While, therefore, the doctrine of Arius evacuated the Atonement of its value, Christ being only a creature, the doctrine of Sabellius stripped it of its meaning and resolved it into only a method of moral influence. This theory did not die with the mob of errors to which the councils gave the death-blow, but its reproductive power lived along with that of Arius, a seed-power, torpid for a while, like the grains of wheat in the cerements of an Egyptian mummy, waiting only for an opening occasion to sprout and bear fruit.

Accordingly, in modern times, Sabellianism has had a fresh birth; first, in Germany, where it met the crazy rationalism of the times and grafted its philosophy upon the religion of the Bible. It was not difficult to do so, for the idea of some sort of trinity in the Godhead was not strange to the old philosophies. Both the Hindoo and the Platonic trinities had entered as elements into the ancient systems of thought, and were, therefore, respectable from their pedigree. Thus Sabellianism had an authentic philosophical footing, which kept it from being despised; and inasmuch as it set forth only a modal Trinity and avoided the puzzling dogma of three persons joined in one substance of nature, its presentment of God had a look no worse than of a religious philosophy, that is, a philosophy that had not so much of religion as to spoil it.

From Germany, the system has crossed the water to England and thence to America, where it lives a popular and advancing life, suiting itself to the class of clerical minds who sympathize with the progressive spirit of the age, and whose young ambition is tinged with intellectuality. The followers of Sabellius do indeed maintain that their doctrine is not forbidden by the church. They claim that the dogmatic teaching of the Nicene creed does not bar them out from the fold of the Orthodox faith, because, while that creed exhausts the very life-blood of Arianism in proclaiming the full divinity of the Son of God, it has no clause that asserts his separate personality. Hence its doctrine of a modal Trinity is not a heresy. This would seem to be at first view a plausible claim. It is not until we refer to the Athanasian creed that Sabellianism meets with an explicit rebuke. In that creed, the most perfect model of dogmatic statement that the world has ever seen, the doctrine of the tri-personality of the Godhead is stated in terms so full and with such discrimination of thought as seem to render a mistake impossible. Its form is not only inclusive, but exclusive as well. Its declarations are antithetical, balanced by an affirmation on one hand and a negation on the other; not only asserting the doctrine but denying in terms its opposite; showing both what it means and what it does not mean at a single glance.

That Creed, therefore, has ever been held to be the best fortified bulwark of the Faith, and, in every church that receives it as authority, the Sabellian belief must be content to hold the place of a tolerated error. Our own Church, by declining to admit it as one of her standards, has left a somewhat open field for the followers of Sabellius to disport their unshackled thoughts. If their theory be not arrested and rebuked by other recognitions of the Trinity in the devotional and liturgical expressions of the Church, there would seem to be nothing in the logical construction of her creeds to convict the other doctrine as illegitimate.

The objections in our day to the doctrine of the Trinity are somewhat different from those of the early times, because they spring from psychological reasoning, a species of thinking unknown to their philosophies. From this source comes the main objection that the doctrine of the tri-personality of God is contradicted by the essential idea of personality, and is therefore necessarily inconceivable and false. The essence of personality, it is said, is self-consciousness, the consciousness of being itself and not another; its function is to create the sense of separateness and individuality and the exclusion of all other individualities.

Now, the doctrine of tri-personality contradicts this elementary self-consciousness; it asserts that the three personalities are one personality, which is to declare that three units are one and the same unit, which is absurd. If we reply that the doctrine does not take the shape of saying three persons in one person, but three persons in one Divine nature, then the objector asks, What is that Divine nature? Is it too a personality? If so, there are four personalities, not three only; and if it be not a personality, but only a nature, an unknown something, then the three persons are independent beings and the system is a Tritheism. What shall we say to this keen and trenchant objection, that pierces to the heart of the doctrine and cuts in twain the silver cord of its vitality?

As the objection is an aggressive one, the answer needs be only defensive. As it makes a positive charge of inconceivability and necessary absurdity, the charge is sufficiently repelled and the doctrine vindicated by a negative. Does the idea of three distinct personal consciousnesses conflict fatally with the idea of the unity of those personalities in one nature? Can any way be shown to the eye of reason in which they may conceivably be joined in a unity of essence without the logical creation of a fourth personal consciousness? In advance of further argument, let me say that perhaps our conclusion may depend somewhat upon the direction in which our minds address the subject.

When the idea of the Trinity is propounded as a philosophical theme, we naturally begin our thinking at the nearest terminus of thought, and reason back to the beginning. We think first of the several personalities, and then proceed to join the severalities into unity, which, after all, is only an aggregation of units, to which we find it difficult to ascribe any subsistence of its own. The connection seems arbitrary and artificial, a union rather than a unity. The doctrine thus takes on the look of tritheism,—the three personalities joined by affinity, and not by constitutional and essential oneness. Supposing, however, that we begin to think at the remoter terminus, and let the conception be of the Godhead as eternally subsisting in a triple form, not compounded of three personalities, but as being never anything else than three. The unity does not then appear as a junction of separate subsistences, but its very constitution and essence is that of a triple subsistence,—an idea which seems to me not beyond the reach of rational conception. If there be a difficulty of thinking this, is not the difficulty one of ignorance rather than of reason, the same that besets all our thoughts of the Divine subsistence, or of any other being or thing, which makes even a blade of grass an enigma, and the whole world a huge, solemn mystery?

But now let us try to meet distinctly the objection that if there be, besides the three personal consciousnesses, another consciousness of the Divine nature itself, then the four consciousnesses are equivalent to four Gods and not three in one. As the whole objection grounds itself in our human psychology, let us get our reply from the same source and take our human consciousness as the basis of thought.

Mankind subsists to-day as twelve hundred millions of distinct personalities, each personality having its distinct consciousness of being itself and not another; yet all these personalities spring from the one ground of nature which we call humanity, binding those personalities together in a characteristic unity which distinguishes them from all other natures, from brute to angelic.

Each one of the personalities contains the whole power and character of human nature as truly and essentially as if it were the only human being in existence. Human nature would not be different, would not be less, if there were only one person to represent it. The plurality of persons, therefore, does not destroy the unity of nature. This will of course be easily admitted, but it will probably be asked, " Is there any consciousness in this nature itself? the consciousness namely among the several persons of being joined together by this common bond ? " " Is there mingled with the personal consciousness, which is the consciousness of separateness, another consciousness, which is the consciousness of unity ? " I think there is. Else what is the meaning of the universal sense of brotherhood? What is that touch of nature that makes the whole world kin ? What is that native sympathy that we feel for the trials and sorrows of mankind, though far away? Why do our hearts sink at their debasement or our blood boil at their wrongs? Why does any distressed man make appeal with a sort of confidence to the generic feelings of human nature? Why does the skilful orator address himself so surely to those generic feelings to gain his cause ? Why is it that companions find themselves so often interpreting each other's silent feelings, anticipating each other's wishes, or uttering at the same moment precisely the same sentiments? Does not this world-known fact imply an underlying consciousness of unity perfectly compatible with the individual consciousness of personality? If so, it seems to me we have analogy enough to warrant the idea of a similar constitution of the Divine nature.

Supposing only the difference of degree between man and God; supposing these facts of our life to be translated into the ineffable conditions of God's life; supposing, in a word, that man, made in the image of God, is a type, no matter how lame and feeble, of the great archetype of infinitude, may we not suppose that the Divine nature may still be distributed into personalities without losing its deity, and at the same time may hold in itself a consciousness of itself, which is incorporated with the consciousness of each personality, pervading each so intimately that with each consciousness of separateness there will be blended the inseparable and intense consciousness of unity? This supposition seems to me perfectly conceivable and answering the essential requirements of the doctrine of the Trinity; and if only conceivable, it meets the objection we are dealing with of impossibility and contradiction. If conceivable, it is not irrational, and if not irrational it may be true. Thus, then, I think the doctrine stands secure from the assaults of human reason, even as, by the confessions of the universal church, it is the fixed truth of revelation. It justifies itself to our acceptance in that not only does the earnest disciple cling to it with his heart, and not only the prolonged strain of Christian consciousness has made this truth, with its dependent truths, the burden of its teaching and its song, but in that our sovereign reason can muster no effective weapons against it, but, standing face to face with the possibility, can only adore the glory of its mystery in the divine Three in One. And this is no skeleton truth: it is clothed with the teguments and filled with the vitality of a practical, spiritual power.

Perhaps it is safe to say that, as it has been the stay and staff of the highest religious life, so without it there had been no abiding Universal Church. It would be an interesting work to show the practical importance of this great truth in detail, to trace its bearings on other revealed truths,— how it works itself in essentially with the atonement of the God-man, how it brightens into life in the agency of the Holy Ghost, the Comforter, and how it thus exalts the whole Christian experience to a higher plane in its faith, its comforts, its strength, and its assured victory.

But the limits of our time forbid such expatiation. I can only suggest that each Christian may educe this rich development in his own personal consciousness, and close with the invocation that the grace of our Lord Jesus Christ, the Eternal Son, the love of God, the Father, and the fellowship of the Holy Ghost, the Comforter, may be with us all, now and evermore. Amen!

LECTURE III.

THE ATONEMENT.

LECTURE III.

THE ATONEMENT.

OUR theme to-night is the doctrine of the atonement of the Lord Jesus Christ. Although we cannot, by searching, find out God, or understand the Almighty to perfection, yet when he himself leaves hanging out from the deep sanctuary where he dwells loops of suggestion to fasten our thoughts upon, our minds will seize them and try to climb up into the mystery of the meaning of things; and although these suggestions be only partial and fragmentary, they may serve to show oftentimes what that meaning is not, though they fail to disclose its full interior force. That the word of God ascribes to the death of Christ an efficacy and importance belonging to the death of no other person, there is of course no question. It stands out in history, with its associated facts, a perfectly unique fact, and its spiritual significance is no less sublimely singular. That significance is that the immortal well-being of our race depends absolutely upon the fact that Jesus Christ died. That the human soul could be saved only through Christ, was the alphabetical faith of Christianity; that salvation was in consequence of Christ's dying, was the next step of supplementary belief.

In this simple form it became the heritage of the generations for two hundred years. The church was not in a condition to deal with theological reasonings. The dogmatic period had not come in. The company of believers had all that they could do to live: to give a reason to their pagan enemies why they should live was often beyond their mental competency. In multitudes of instances they could only say, " I believe," and then die. Perhaps we can measure the extent of their faith in Christ's atonement from the instance of Philip and the Eunuch in the Acts of the Apostles. The Eunuch was reading from the Prophet Isaiah, " He was led as a lamb to the slaughter, and as the sheep before her shearer is dumb, so opened he not his mouth." The context of these words is, He hath borne our griefs and carried our sorrows. He was wounded for our transgressions, he was bruised for our iniquities; the chastisement of our peace was upon him, and by his stripes we are healed. "Of whom speaketh the Prophet this," said the Eunuch, "of himself or of some other man?" Then Philip began at the same place, and preached unto him Jesus,—Jesus, as the fulfilment of that stirring prophecy, suffering, but not for himself, innocent of all wrong but bearing the sins of many, wounded and bruised like a criminal, not for his own transgression, but for ours. The Eunuch accepted this gospel, was baptized in its faith, and went on his way rejoicing. It was gospel enough for the salvation of a world, and the faith of the simple fact of Christ's death could transform the unhappy heart of sin into a fountain of peace and joy. The essential element of this belief lay in the vicariousness of Christ's suffering. Whatever he endured was as a substitute for sinners. Believing this, they asked not how or why; they rested in no formula of words, but in the personal, divine, dying Christ, whose death was their life. By this they lived and died. But when the dogmatic period dawned, the Church began to think out explanations and to form theories of the Atonement, and in doing so they would pitch upon some word of Scripture which signified the character of the Atonement, and that word would be made the germ point of a theory. There were many such words, and each one denoted a distinct aspect of the atoning work.

Redemption, mediation, sacrifice, purchase, propitiation, ransom,—a theory built on either of these words alone was pretty sure to run into some impracticable conclusion; and even to join them together was to make the theory loose-jointed and incongruous. These descriptive words all agreed, however, in one essential meaning; they all denoted something done by one person for and in behalf of another person; the element of vicariousness was wrapped up in them all. Of these suggestive words the word "ransom" seems to have seized the minds of the age the earliest. They knew what ransom meant, the buying back from slavery, because it was the daily usage of all the peoples of the earth, and they adopted the idea as the prime element of Christ's atonement. But then the question came, From whom did Christ buy back the lost race of men? Who was their master and what was the slavery? The slavery, it was answered, is sin, and the enslaving power is Satan; hence the great ransom was paid to God's prime enemy, the Prince of Evil. He had snatched the jewel souls of men from the diadem of the Almighty, and by the laws of conquest they were his, unless their former owner and creator should buy them back by some equivalent, and that equivalent was his Son's life, rendered up under such circumstances of agony and woe as, while Heaven mourned, the arch-fiend triumphed. To our ears such a statement has the sound of a shriek, a discord of horror and absurdity; yet it was the favorite theory for a thousand years,—not unbroken by protest and denial, but with enough of continuity to make a chain of great names in its support. I cannot recite the objections that led to its overthrow, but they are such as rise up in our Christian thoughts much more easily than in minds whose thinking was done for them, and which knew nothing of the Bible,—the generations of the Dark

Ages. It might seem to have sprung from the Manichean philosophy, which held a dualism in the government of the world,—good and bad powers equally independent and always contending for sovereignty.

The empire of this theory, which had run through ages of secularism and corruption in the church, was broken by Anselm, Archbishop of Canterbury, in the early part of the twelfth century.

In his great book entitled "Why God became Man," he lifted the whole conception of Christ's atonement into the blended light of the essential deity and the essential humanity, and showed that, as man's first, last misery was personal guiltiness, so his first, last, total want was the blotting out of that guiltiness, the free and absolute forgiveness of his sins. Christ therefore made propitiation to the Father, not to Satan, and the Father, who would otherwise be held back from forgiveness by the sanction of his holiness, justice, and truth, could now pronounce his law, which embodied all the three, satisfied and vindicated.

Mercy and Truth met together, Righteousness and Peace kissed each other at the cross when

Jesus died. God could now be just and still justify the ungodly. This theory of Anselm's was argued with immense force of logic, and with that knowledge of human nature which comes from profound religious experience, holding the heart up between itself and God, so that in his divine light a man sees himself as in a transparency. But not even the great power and piety of Anselm could gain supremacy for his theory at once. It lived a checkered life up to the sixteenth century, —the period of the Reformation,—when it became the accepted type of religious thinking among the most strenuous thinkers of the most strenuous age of history. The emancipation of the human mind which sprang of that grand epoch, the depth of spiritual insight begotten of the free reading of God's word, the vigor of the whole manhood of man which came up into consciousness under the stimulating force of freedom, were mainly centred on religious themes.

The influence of the schoolmen in sharpening the thinking powers had prepared the way for the handling of deep and abstract topics, and there were none others to challenge their thoughts.

The brilliant era of material science was full two centuries in the future. Bacon was not yet born to discover or recover the master-key of induction which was to unlock the penetralia of Nature, so that men could enter, and explore her open secrets. Hence the accumulated thought of the age threw its whole weight into theology, canvassing and criticising its deep revelations, and none so much as the central one of Christ's redeeming work, its methods and its power, how it could obviate the moral demerit of man and procure the pardon of his sins.

Men saw that this was the pivot truth of revelation; that the whole gospel was gathered into it; that if there were no substitute to bear the retribution of man's guilt, there was to human conceptions no assignable reason why there should be a gospel at all, with its tremendous sacrifice of a humiliated God. The gospel would be then only a reduplication of the religion of nature, with the addition of the Divine Person to reinforce the testimony of the Divine works.

Martin Luther, with his intense soul, seized upon the divinity of the atonement with such an absolute embrace as seemed almost to neutralize the responsibility of man. Christ was the believer's substituted righteousness, not only by what he endured, but likewise by what he did; his active as well as his passive obedience were in the place and in behalf of man's. His theory seemed to involve the conclusion that since, because Christ suffered for human sin, man need not suffer, so if Christ obeyed for man, then man need not obey. It was charged with unhinging the code of moral sanctions, and inaugurating a saturnalia of licentiousness. But Luther repelled the vicious conclusion by replying that although the law of obedience was blotted out by the blood of Christ, yet the new Christ life of the believer was its own inspired and instinctive law. Obedience would grow out of him instead of being forced upon him.

The Lutheran doctrine became essentially the doctrine of all the reformed churches, though modified by various theories touching the method of the atonement, each theory being met by specific objections. The theories all agreed, however, in maintaining the idea of substitution as the characteristic and vital element of the atoning work, so that with the body of believers there was a substantial unity of faith.

We can easily understand to what classes of religious thinkers the fundamental idea of substitution would be absolutely repulsive. The Arian, who denied the divinity of Christ, would of course refuse assent to the idea throughout, since it was absurd to suppose that a created being could offer a meritorious satisfaction for the sins of a world.

The Sabellian, maintaining that Christ was only the Father with another name, must likewise deny the substitution, because it is impossible to think of the same person offering sacrifice and propitiation to himself.

The Arian views were represented by Socinus, the lineal predecessor of the Unitarians; but the Sabellian theory of the Trinity had not then, so far as I know, any class representative. The revival of Sabellianism was of later date. Its reappearance is, indeed, an event of our century, and it occurred, not so much as a lapse from the true belief as a recoil from the dreary, dark denial of Christianity itself, which involved the churches of Germany, through several generations. The Germans had translated into their own tongue the writings of the English deists of the seventeenth century, and had transformed their matter-of-fact unbelief into the sublimated speculations that characterize the Teutonic thinking. Their scepticism took the form of a philosophy which culminated in pantheism, rejecting the Bible entirely, or else trying to square its statements with their philosophy, and torturing the sacred writings by interpretations of melancholy grotesqueness. From such a system of madly independent thought, a doctrine like that of the atonement would of necessity drop out; and while the Church was dominated by the Schools, and its ministers were of their training, the former faith became, with few exceptions, a dead orthodoxy. Here and there was heard a solitary and gentle reclaim from some whose religious consciousness could not quite be obscured by the philosophical fog, men of fervid piety, but with such an overruling influence of their academic training that it seems almost as if their philosophy was their gospel after all.

Schleiermacher represents most truly this partial return of faith from the wild verge to which it had run, and with him and his sanctified philosophy, Christianity became respectable again, and Christ a power; but even with him it is not Christ, the sacrifice, the propitiation, the High Priest, but Christ, the loving and living Son of God, coming down to draw men to himself by the attractions of his spiritual loveliness and by the fulness with which he meets the soul's aspiration after God.

Beautiful, fascinating as this sort of faith is, it fails, evidently, to reach the deep relation of Christ to our moral nature, which our nature, awakened to its utter need, feels even to the centre of its consciousness. This system is, however, so clear an advance from the dead sea of philosophical unbelief towards the promised land of God's people, that the Christian faith may thank God and take courage, with the hope of a restored, believing Germany.

The German philosophy, in its improved form, was borrowed into England by Coleridge, and was set forth by him to a school of thoughtful disciples, numbering men of the purest character and of the finest minds in the realm. His influence was that of an oracle, speaking sometimes as from the glory of an open firmament of light and sometimes from the darkness of a clouded sky, but always with an authority that seemed to come down from above. Almost the whole school of his disciples were led by him into a style of religious thinking that sank the cross out of its singular eminence. The propitiatory element of the doctrine of the atonement was volatilized, and escaped. The idea of substitution was rejected; "vicarious" became an ill-sounding word; the ground-work of atonement, as laid in the moral guiltiness of man, was covered up. "Guilt" seemed a word of another vocabulary. Man's sinfulness was represented as very much a misfortune, but as hardly more. God's love was presented as the attributes which engrossed and concealed the other attributes in its own bosom of light; his holiness, his justice, his truth, were not considered as leading powers in his administrative relations with man. Judgment and the retributions of a life after this seemed to be practically disallowed, and God, as a moral administrator, the Deity of an obsolete dispensation. His character was displayed as a pure fatherliness. In fact, it was customary to say that the single purpose of the mission of the Son of God was to proclaim the fatherhood of God as a truth of glory hitherto unrevealed.

To the common definition of atonement the constant reply was that atonement means reconciliation, and that of the two parties at variance God needs no reconciliation. His fatherly heart is already bending itself towards the wickedest, and it is man alone who needs to be influenced and changed. To awaken or create the temper of reconciliation in the human soul Christ came in mighty humiliation, was incarnated, taught, endured a life of cruel self-denial, which, by its persuasive pathos, might subdue the hard unwillingness that kept man from God. To this life of sorrow and wretchedness his death was only the apt and necessary conclusion. And all this, his life as much as his death, was his atonement.

Next to this it follows that, to become a Christian, a man must tread in the footsteps of Christ, obey his precepts, especially imitating the daily self-denial of the Saviour, and so achieving for himself a Christly character. In all this the sacrificial character of Christ's death is impatiently set aside with the grouped thoughts that gathered to it from before and behind,—man's guilt and helpless doom, the life-giving power of faith in a Divine substitute of doom, the Holy Spirit's help covenanted by the atoning death, and the final acceptance of the soul with God,—accepted in the beloved. I have called this the Sabellian view of the atonement, not because all who hold it must necessarily be Sabellians, but because the Sabellian doctrine of the Trinity will harmonize with no other doctrine of the atonement except this. It is a doctrine that has grown and is growing with the Century, in England and in America, in the English Church and in our own. It numbers among its teachers and preachers bright and pure men, whose elevated lives seem to vouch, as far as a life can vouch, for the truth of their doctrine. As it was in the case of Arius and Apollinarius, and with our early Unitarians, so was it with the Brothers Hare, and with Maurice and Robertson and Stanley and Dr. John Young in England, and with Bushnell in America. Before we investigate the causes that have given birth and vigorous currency to this theory, let us test some of its positions by the Scriptures. I think that its foremost assertion that Christ came to proclaim the fatherhood of God, hitherto an unacknowledged truth, is an assertion that lacks the warranty of the Word of God. I am not sure that the Old Testament has fewer declarations of God's paternal character than the New, and if it has, I am sure that those declarations are so emphatic, and their illustrations so subduingly tender, that none can be more so. The Concordance will show how often the gracious title is employed. The Psalms reveal the fatherhood in such winning guise that Jesus seems to have adopted it as the illustration of his own loving nurture of his flock. The whole twenty-third Psalm is full of the fatherhood. That it was not a fatherhood of the Jews alone, but of all mankind, was recognized by the prophet,—"Doubtless thou art our father, though Abraham be ignorant of us."

The first postulate of the theory, therefore, seems to be too hastily assumed. Take next the statement that Christ's whole life was one of painful self-denial, which was a chief element of the persuasive reconciling power that lay in his life's suffering as much as in the pains of his death.

This statement, again, seems hardly to be borne out by the narrative of the four Gospels; for up to his thirtieth year, Jesus lived the common life of his family and friends, with no more than the usual trials of an humble condition of life, the economy of a community not rich. In that year he commenced his ministry with his baptism. Then the Father's word came down from the open heaven to warrant his commission of Messiahship,—" This is my beloved Son in whom I am well pleased." Then the Holy Ghost descended upon him to endow him with the full spirit and power of Messiahship, and filling him then, for the first time, with its ripe consciousness, leads him into the wilderness to hold for forty days transcendent and delighted communion with his Father,—communion so transcendent that its rapture absorbed all consciousness of physical want. Afterwards he was an hungered, and Satan came upon his exhausted frame and tortured it with temptations; but even in his exhaustion his new-born consciousness of power defeated the Tempter with a word. Here is the first thing that can be called a pain in Christ's life, if that may be called a pain which was the occasion of such easy, divine victory: it was no self-denial, but the calm superiority of the spirit over matter, of heaven over earth. We cannot conceive of his being for an instant in doubt, or of his conscience wavering for a moment from its heavenward poise. True, he learned what the power of Satan must be over us, his frail brotherhood, and he taught us too that thereby he was fitted to be a sympathizing intercessor with the Father, and that we should conquer even as he conquered.

For three years after this he lived the life of a pilgrim, with no home of his own, but not without friends whose home was his, and never in all the time complaining of any material hardship or trial. But as the time of his death approached, there came the agony of heart and soul in Gethsemane that made him the very prophetic "Man of sorrows, acquainted with grief." Yet this sorrow was associated, not with his life, but with the atoning death he was to die,—a shadow of its gloom in advance. There would seem to have been no other real sorrow of Christ, none that a genuine, generous manhood would not refuse to call such, except those divine human griefs, inaccessible to human conception, which made at once the indescribable woe and the unutterable glory of the cross. To affirm self-denial in the life of Christ as a pain and a torment seems to be as unworthy of him as it is untrue to Scripture. To say that his life, equally with his death, made part of his suffering for man, is to ignore the open passages where his redemption is centred in the one point of his dying. "Redemption through His blood, even the forgiveness of sins," is the brief formula which conveys, in whatever variations, the truth that the atonement was concentred at the cross. It sounds out in the various language of the Bible, and it sounds down from the song of the redeemed. And more yet, when Christ himself would show us how he would have us hold the faith, he embodied it in a memorial sacrament exhibiting the concrete of the gospel, the unchanging type of Christian belief,—his body and his blood, his death, not his life.

Again, the theory that we are canvassing declares that Christ came to illustrate the divine love, and so to persuade men to repentance. Dr. Bushnell explains it thus: A person who has inflicted an injury upon another is apt to imagine him to be in a state of chronic resentment; hence he is suspicious of him and avoids him. If overtures of reconciliation are made, he suspects their sincerity; if he is assured that the feelings of the injured person are still kindly and complacent, he cannot be made to believe it. And so, fearing a latent resentment burrowing in the heart of his enemy, he dares not put himself within its reach and keeps off in estrangement and hostility.

So is it, says Dr. Bushnell, with man and God. Man, being the offender, supposes God to be his enemy; hence he avoids him, is afraid of him. If he believed that God truly loved him, it would melt down the iron of his impenitence and bring him into a state of reconciliation. To convince him of his love, God blesses him with the good things of his Providence; and as man still doubts, God sends him special messages in his Word, assuring him of his abiding paternal tenderness; and when, after all, man still holds in his bosom, like a demon, the infesting doubt, God comes down himself, and dies on the cross, to show the supreme strength of his love, proving by symbol what he had already declared by word. The death of Christ, therefore, removes no impediment in the way of man's forgiveness. It makes no retributive exaction upon his wilful guilt; it tells him to come back to the Father he has left, and all will be well; it adds no new truth, but reaffirms in a new way an old one. The mighty tragedy of the cross is an exhibition, arranged on purpose as an exhibition.

There is a histrionic air in the transaction as thus explained that carries to the mind an impression of unreality, and robs the dreadful death of all the persuasive power that is ascribed to it. It seems painstaking and artificial, an ingenious expedient to produce an emotional effect; and when it has done this, the whole force and meaning of the cross is exhausted. That supreme crisis in the history of God's dealings with our apostate mankind, which had been the theme of agonized and of joyous prophecy through the ages, which was to solve the heavenly problem that angels desired to look into,—" how God could be just and yet justify the ungodly,"—the grand event which began with the humiliation of God and went on controlling the course of affairs, public and private, and leading the whole order of Divine Providence in its train, so that it became the focal point to which the natural and moral attributes of God had long tended, and were now centred as to a finality, a consummation, beyond which there could be nothing more,—this crowning crisis was after all to be only a display, showing nothing that man did not know before, but only asserting it in such a way and with such an avowed purpose of display as to impair its moral influence, and to put the mind into a critical mood that would of itself drive the sensibilities back into inaccessibility. The great experiment on human feeling would thus inevitably precipitate its own failure. It is most different, I think, to all this when the death of the Son of God is the propitiation for the guilt of the world, a penal death that bore on its broad substitution the sins of mankind, meeting the demands of eternal truth and righteousness, and abolishing human guilt forever. That death is no mere display, not a simple method of persuasion. It does something; it reverses the moral condition of man, changes it from dark doom to hope and cheer.

It is indeed an exhibition of Divine love, but not of love proposing and preparing itself for exhibition alone. The love is seen in its purpose and its results,—Christ dying to save us from dying, dying once for all, that we need not die eternally. "Herein is love, that God gave his Son to be the propitiation for our sins." When the Divine love comes out into this light it comes with a persuasive force as strong as the felt value of the soul. It is not what the cross seems, but what it does, that makes it a power. If the soul can ever be subdued and reclaimed to God by the death of Christ, it is when it sees in that death the redeeming purchase of its own forfeited life, the blood-bought pardon of its guilt. Then it is a power of regeneration that grasps the soul around, and holds it in the delighted embrace of God and his salvation. Upon this point, namely, the comparative efficacy of the two theories of the atonement in meeting the wants of the soul in its most awakened life, we may refer even to Dr. Bushnell himself, a witness of authority, who, in his work on Vicarious Atonement, makes a concession against his own principles as remarkable, perhaps, as anything in all literature.

After elaborating the Sabellian theory of the atonement throughout nearly his whole volume, with his accustomed vigor of argument and rhetoric, he passes in one of the closing chapters to consider its value and power as an experimental truth, and compares it with the accepted doctrine of the atonement, which he calls the "Altar Theory." In this comparison he frankly admits that to a person oppressed with the convictions of conscience and the sense of guiltiness, his theory ministers no solace. It does not satisfy the instinctive perception of righteousness, which is always strongest and clearest in a soul convicted of its own unrighteousness, and which always joins together sin and retribution as necessary correlatives. The "Altar View" alone will meet and satisfy the cravings of that awakened and conscience-stricken person. Christ must be presented to him as a sacrifice, oblation, and satisfaction for his sins, and then, renouncing all other trust, he rests upon the merit of a dying Saviour, and finds the surpassing peace of pardon through his blood. On reading this strange admission, one can hardly help asking, "If the author knew the worthlessness of his theory

before he wrote his book, why did he write it?
If he did not know it till the book was written,
why did he publish it?"

This theory chimes in, no doubt, with the humanitarianism of the age, which thinks more of compassion than of justice and righteousness. The engrossment of our philanthropy confines our contemplations so much to the earth and its wants, that we fail to look up to the heavens, and to Him who dwelleth therein. Man's wants and poverty lead us to overlook man's crimes, till we come to feel that God will overlook them too; and when once the sense and appreciation of guilt goes out, all the grand, grave truths of the Bible that postulate that guilt must fail of access to the consciousness of men.

The prosperity and self-indulgence of the times, the triumph of scientific thought, the skill of our arts, the pride of our freedom, all conspire to make man the all in all, and God the ready servitor. The Bible grows into disuse, and then into disrespect; its theology is discarded as narrow, its solemn sanctions as null. It is as if, in our self-sufficiency, the general mind had been drugged with henbane, and through its dilated pupil saw everything only broad and dim.

Turning from the criticism of theories, let us consider a question often asked, " What is the test quality by which, among all the theories of the atonement, we may know the true one,—the one maintained in the Christian consciousness of the ages?" I suppose the true answer to be that whatever theory recognizes the death of Christ as a reason or an influence, on account of which God grants us the grace of his forgiveness, such is essentially a true doctrine of the atonement. If, on the other hand, the theory represents the death of Christ as having no effect Godward, but only as a moral power, a divine persuasive to man's soul, then, though Christ be exhibited in the fascination of his living person, the beauty of his benevolence, and the whole varied loveliness of his life, or be presented as a martyr dying for the truth, and the dying be tinged with such pathos that we pity and weep, and are aroused and are indignant, all at once, yet if there be no more than this, the theory fails of that Scriptural accord without which it is a fallacy. At this point the road forks, and while the one theory holds the soul to Christ, and leads the church to God, higher and nearer as the road leads forward, the other theory has none but a descending advance, the farther the lower, until it may reach the common terrestrial level where Christ is no better than Socrates, or the Gospel than the Memorabilia. Although I have discussed our theme at such length, I am loath to let it go.

Among the diverse theories which hold the essential idea of atonement, is there any one which commends itself specially as denoting the true method? To my mind, there is one grandly peculiar and satisfying to the human consciousness of guilt. I can do hardly more than suggest it. It is grounded on the strange, heart-stirring cry of Christ upon the cross, "My God, my God! Why hast thou forsaken me?" These words admit of no rhetorical gloss. It were monstrous to torture them by a various reading. They are a live picture of Christ's consciousness. He was forsaken of his Father. We may not analyze his condition of mind, but it must have been pure woe. The filial consciousness of the Divine Son towards the

Divine Father was broken. He was as an alien. If this be so, then we can understand the only real woe that ever came near to the soul and life of Christ. It was the very woe he came to bear; it was the culminating point of his redeeming work. For this cause came he to this hour. It was the cup his Father had given him, and he drank it. And whence and why this woe? the soul reverently asks. Was this a penal woe? It was either this or else gratuitous cruelty. It was penal, then; but penal on whose account? He did no sin. Look at it a moment, and remember that God's desertion is the specific doom of sin. "Depart from me" is the formulated woe of eternity; and that woe, the precise penalty of human guilt, was precisely forestalled upon the cross. He bore our sins and carried our sorrows; he was our very substitute in penal suffering. "Thou shalt make his soul an offering for sin.' Can we go any further? Perhaps so. The Son of God—the eternal *Logos* —was the Creator and the light and life of men. His being was incorporated with human life before he was born of Mary. His incarnation was the symbol of a foregone and still subsisting fact that the Son of God and humanity were life of life. Everything that Christ did, he did for man in man's place as man, man's representative. In the agony of the garden humanity suffered with him; on the cross humanity cried out; in that penal woe, to which Christ gave his consenting soul, humanity was bearing its penalty. He acted and suffered for us, and we by him. It was by no fiction of law, by no technical relation, that he was our surety and our substitute: he was our very selves. In him humanity bowed itself to the infliction, owned its perfect righteousness, and was restored to a divine sonship. A soul may still reluct, resist, rebel; but when it turns to God at last, it claims affiance with the dying Elder Brother of the race, echoes his cry of agony as if it were its own cry, consents as he consented, and feels and knows that the great satisfaction has been made in its divine fulness, and that henceforth there is no condemnation.

This may be the true method of atonement, yet whether true or not, we know it is not the method, but the glorious fact itself, on which our faith must rest; and resting there, we are prepared to glorify our Redeemer by an ever-adoring service of gratitude here on earth, and to join in the song of the saved above, " Worthy the Lamb" who has redeemed us to God by his blood!

LECTURE IV.

THE HOLY GHOST.

LECTURE IV.

THE HOLY GHOST.

FOR this fourth lecture I take for my subject "The Holy Ghost, the Lord and Giver of life." So the subject is designated in the creed.

The triple personality of the Godhead is not a truth without its fruits. We are taught that in the economy of the Divine administration each personality has its distinct function and agency,— the Father as the prime administrator, with whom is authority, counsel, and direction; the Son, the eternal *Logos*, as the expressive power the manifester of God, whether by word or life, whether before or after his incarnation; and the Holy Ghost as the practical energy of Deity, to make effectual the Divine counsels by living results through all the realms of creation and with all classes of created things. When we speak of the works of God, therefore, we define the specific agency and power of the Holy Ghost. Whatever of omnipotence, of omniscience, or of omnipresence is involved in producing and maintaining the universe, is the working power of Deity through the third person of the Godhead.

Thus the whole amplitude of the world is opened out before us. Its manifold forms of subsistence come into review one by one; for he is the giver of life to them all, and their presiding Lord as well.

We begin, therefore, with the physical creation, of which the Scriptural account runs thus: " In the beginning God created the heaven and the earth, and the earth was without form and void, and darkness was upon the face of the deep. And the Spirit of God moved upon the face of the waters. And God said, Let there be light, and there was light."

Of course a description like this will have to encounter what are called the discoveries of modern science which claim to have exploded this whole history of the creation as partly a fallacy and the rest an absurdity. The alleged absurdity lies in supposing, as this account seems to suppose, that God created something out of nothing, whereas it is an axiom of science that nothing can ever be produced from nothing. Now this axiom is brought down to us from the ancient philosophies, in which a personal Creator had no recognized place. It is a maxim which gauges the possibilities of things by a simply human standard. No skill of man could ever produce something out of nothing, and no wit of man, which can affirm only from experience, can understand how it can be done; and so it is peremptorily affirmed to be impossible.

The weakness of the objection lies in its leaving out the presence and power of a Creator, who is infinitely greater than man, and who, for aught that we know, can perform an act of pure and simple creation, bringing entity out of non-entity.

There is no self-contradiction in the statement.

The difficulty lies in our not being able to conceive how it can be done, and this difficulty besets all our thinking when we think about the works of God. This objection, grounded in our ignorance, ought not to claim the dignity of an argument, still less assume the authority of a universal denial of possibility. Though founded on an accredited axiom of science, it is plainly unphilosophical and beyond the modesty of reason.

Moreover, to deny the possible creation of something out of nothing is to assert the eternity of material substance, distinct from the nature and substance of God,—a theory which involves several rational difficulties.

For if matter be eternal, then its existence must be a necessary existence, which is self-existence that cannot be impaired or modified by any other power. It must be endued with all the essential attributes of infinitude,—a deity in and of itself, a rival of God, ever at war with him, unless one or the other God parts with some of his attributes, which, since each exists, not of his own will, but by necessity, neither can do.

It is the old Manichean notion, long since adjudged a fallacy by the consenting reason of mankind.

Assuming, then, the creation of crude amorphous matter, without form and void of organic life, we are told that "the Spirit of God moved upon the face of the waters."

The expression beautifully denotes a hovering, brooding action, as if shedding down upon the fluid mass a generative power, when all at once went forth the life-giving fiat, "Let there be light," and the world became charged with the diffusive energy, "light was."

It may be interesting to inquire how far the verified statements of science can be made to square with this history of creation. Accepting as the last discovery of Scientific research the existence of a substance, protoplasm or bioplasm, which forms the basis of all organic life (although all scientific men do not admit its universality), accepting, likewise, its wonderful microscopic developments, its corpuscles, monads, cells, and atoms, we are all aglow with the enthusiasm of discovery. We seem to be penetrating the grand secret of universal existence. Yet presently we are arrested by an impracticability. We have not found the source of life; we have only reached the microscopic limit of form. Every one of these atoms of matter is itself an organized substance, moulded and combined of simpler elements by virtue of that life-power which is alone the producer of organism.

Whence is that life-power, the grand, universal motor from which all organic life is begotten? "Grant me," says a chief Priest of Science,—"grant me only a particle of protoplasm and the merest scintilla of force, and with time enough I can evolve the universe." Most true; but we cannot grant it unless science can discover it. It would not be scientific to do so. And if it be not granted, then how stands the problem?

Force, the power of motion, is a thing entirely foreign to matter. Matter is inert and eternally at rest, unless moved from without, and, we add, from above, from the great personal will that, in the person of the Divine Spirit, broods upon the vapory chaos which Science itself teaches to have been the first loose form of things, and, with one stroke of force, sets the elements to work producing atoms, cells, monads, and diffused bioplasm, until the chaos becomes a kosmos. How congruous, then, with scientific suggestion is the Scripture history of creation,—"Let there be light," and light was. As was explained in my first lecture, science has demonstrated the beautiful truth of the correlation of forces, showing that light and heat and electricity and magnetism, and the rest are congeners and may work a common office, and that any one of them, by whatever name it be called, may replace the rest, and produce the organic results of creation.

The parent force of this family of forces is, according to the present tendency of scientific opinion, simple motion, which, like a living centre, radiates and evolves itself into the various forms of material energy. Accepting this conclusion, we see the Divine volition impinging, at a stroke, on the chaotic mass, and producing what our common experience proves to be the first result of volition, viz., motion, the action and interaction of the material elements upon each other, establishing the immediate play of affinities, working instant combinations of form, and, throughout the mighty stir, attesting itself in a flash of universal light. "Let there be light" is the word-form of the Almighty volition; "there was light" denotes its outcome into visible effect.

As the eye answers at a glance to the summons received by the ear, so the flashing world responded on the instant to the spoken will of God. To human conception the volition, the resulting motion, and the attesting light would be simultaneous, without gap or pause for a single interposing thought. Therefore, the suddenness implied in the Scripture account of creation is no objection to its truth.

The entrance of force must always be instantaneous. No matter how slow and complicated the antecedent conditions of life, there is a moment when life is not; and there is another and next moment when it is. The quickening act is a dart, a thrill, a stroke of force, whose effect is not a production from itself, but the presence of itself. The power begotten is the simple transfer of the power begetting. Hence the scientific truth, as well as the rhetorical sublimity, of the creative fiat,— "Let there be light, and there was light."

"I believe in the Holy Ghost the Lord" as well as "the Giver of life." That is, the material creation is still under the daily regulating power of the Creator.

The minds of men have been long divided on the question whether the Divine superintendence of the world is indeed a present fact. Did God, when he set the universe in motion, establish for it a self-regulating system of laws, and leave it to run on, like a clock, to its assigned terminus of duration, and then withdraw himself into the seclusion of his self-existence; or is he present in every movement? Is every movement of things, no matter how minute, the impulse of a distinct volition of Omnipotence, so that the changing play of atoms, the delicate interlacing of affinities, and every miscroscopic vibration shall be the products of so many mental purposes of the universal wisdom? The former theory—that God has retired from the immediate direction of the universe into a calm self-subsistence—has the look of Buddha about it; it suggests a changeless fate; it bars out the fatherhood; it forbids a miracle or a Providence; it chills the spontaneous gratitude that comes from feeling God in nature and life; it makes our moral pilgrimage a cheerless, dreary, dreadful way.

It is the preferred theory of Science, however; and making the world everything and God nothing, establishing law as having no interfering lawgiver, Science can the more courageously speculate to conclusions in which the idea of a personal God is as a cipher. If Science would admit the conception of him as the present Lord as well as the first Giver of life, how would the glitter of her several discoveries gather a mellow beauty, as they flashed forth from amidst the great cloud of glory that embodies the infinite Godhead!

But touching the second theory that God works by his immediate presence, even in the minutest phenomena of nature, it is objected that it seems impossible to be conceived, and that it belittles the conception of him to our minds, to think of him as among the atoms of things.

It is impossible to be conceived, because omnipresence is inconceivable, while yet it is very true. But, granting omnipresence, God's instant power may be very naturally a fact: and if we try to suppose the opposite, I think we find it very difficult to conceive how his power can be where his presence is not. Then, as to the belittling impression it conveys of God, we should remember that to the Infinite One there is no great and no small; great things are contained in small; the vast telescopic universe is composed of the microscopic atoms. It seems more worthy of God that he should be the Lord of life; and Science will become a benefactor to the soul of man when she shall admit God's presence with his power, so that not a sparrow falls to the ground without our Father, and that he numbers the very hairs of our heads. Such is the agency and power of the Holy Spirit among material things,—giver and director of the life of the physical world.

But he has a higher realm than this. All animated things come forth from him, and chiefly does he hold communion with, and interpenetrate with his own life the life of man,—man's intellect, his conscience, his affections, and his will. Some of these communications of the Spirit bear the character of miracle, specially when he imparts to the human mind the power of prophesying. The creed distinguishes this agency thus, "the Holy Ghost who spake by the prophets."

There is no exercise of the reason of man in which it so soon finds the limits of its power as when it undertakes to forecast the future of things.

In the loose connections of daily life and in Politics and Political Economy and Finance, where the calculations of the closet may be disturbed and tossed into confusion by any sidelong accident it was impossible to detect, this failure is not so strange; but even in the exacter sciences, where material laws are fixed and well understood, the failure is hardly less flagrant. The wisest Medical skill will fail in its predictions almost as often as the guess of the empiric. The best scientist of his time pronounced the impossibility of navigating the Atlantic by steamers at the very moment when the first steamship was on her bounding way to the opposite continent.

Whenever Science parts with its abstractness, and mixes itself with the moving concrete of practical life, it so far forfeits its certainty. Its highest, its sole achievement is to know what is. God has not granted it as a normal attainment of the human intellect to read the future. Hence it is that the gift of prophecy has always been regarded as a a miraculous endowment, attesting a divine influence, and to the possessor of the gift men have bowed down with reverence and prayers and rich gifts.

We need not touch the question of the pagan oracles, with their equivocal pronouncements and the clinging suspicion of collusion. We are speaking of the Holy Ghost as he spake by the prophets of the elder Scriptures. Those Scriptures are remarkable for nothing so much as for their prophecy. They are a chain of forecasting testimonies, uttered with assurance, and in some cases depicting the future with such vivid distinctness that our imaginations can sketch the scene as a transaction before our eyes.

Now these prophecies were mainly concerned with the character and biography of one single person, the promised Messiah, whose history was so unique, abounding in incidents so far outside the usual current of events, that a single prophecy, touching only a few of such events, if it should be verified by a fulfilment, would be lifted far above the level of a lucky guess, and might claim inspiration for its origin. But the strangeness is almost infinitely enhanced when we consider the vast variety of particulars that were to centre in the life of that coming man, Jesus of Nazareth, some of them almost self-contradictory and unwarranted by the accepted principles of human nature and the laws of probability.

To show how far towards the infinite the strangeness of fulfilment truly reached, I borrow the statement of the eminent mathematician, Dr. Olinthus Gregory.

Suppose there had been only ten men professing to be prophets, and that each one of the ten should fix upon only five independent criteria touching place, government, events, doctrine, character, sufferings, or death of one particular person; then, according to the principles employed by mathematicians in reference to the doctrine of chances, the probability against the happening of these fifty particulars in any way is that of the fiftieth power of two to unity, that is, the probability is greater than eleven hundred and twenty-five millions of millions to one that all these circumstances do not turn up even at distinct periods.

Now, if to this computation we add the element of time, and consider that any of these predictions might, on the principle of chance, take place from the time of the prophecy to the end of the world, then the chance of their happening at the time predicted would be so unlikely that it surpasses the power of numbers to express the improbability. Can we say less, then, touching the Messianic predictions, than that the Holy Ghost spake by the Prophets?

As we read those prophecies we cannot avoid thinking that "holy men spake as they were moved," not knowing always the pregnancy of what they spake, sometimes with an unconsciously double sense, looking along the line from the typical fact before their eyes to the great antitypical event on which the prophecy terminated, sometimes speaking with coolness and deliberation, at other times wrapt into an abnormal state by the vision and the faculty divine, yet uttering with their human lips the eternal mind of God.

But the Holy Ghost has other ways besides the Prophetic way of laying himself alongside the mind of man, and giving form and pressure to his thoughts and mental instincts. In the awakening of high moral conceptions, and the stirring of the motive powers of the soul to reach out for their fulfilment, opening before its lifted eye a surpassing realm of purity and love and unchecked moral power, to become its own in a life after death,— such things have come into men's lives as powers, not homeborn, but foreign and divine. Socrates seems to have been conscious of it daily. His demon of good, was it not the directing Holy Ghost?

The Holy Ghost again rules in that supernal region of man's nature, the region of the moral sense. Conscience is indeed the throne of the Holy Ghost. It is the regal faculty whose divinity no man ever dared deny. Whenever he heard the voice of the grand moral imperative and looked within, he was sure to stand face to face with the Holy Ghost.

If he thwarted his conscience, defied it, even crucified it, he has always felt that his antagonism was rebellion and that he had crucified his king. The function of this Divine Spirit is to touch the cords of the moral nature, and to keep its sensibility awake to the issues of good and evil. It is He who probes the peccant parts of the soul to make us feel how deep the sinuous ulcer runs. He detains our rambling fancies, and makes us think with an inner concentration that shall beget a better self-knowledge. He shows us right and wrong aloof from those mixed tints of life that make sin seem attractive, and reveals to us the white light of righteousness, that we can see how unshadedly bright is good, and how deadly black, without a ray of relieving light, is sin. It is in this way, by its clear marking of moral distinctions to the soul through the illuminated conscience, that the Holy Ghost prepares the way for his covenanted and commissioned agency as the representative of Christ.

"He shall take of the things of mine," says the Saviour, "and shall show them unto you." In order to this, in order to prepare an entrance for the Great Salvation, to create a loathing of unrighteousness, and a longing in the soul for a perfect emancipation from its power, the conscience must be both enlightened and sensitive. And then, when, possessed by the alternate loathing and longing, it cries, What shall I do? the indwelling Spirit reveals the cross and the Crucified, and imparts to the vague feelings definite shape and quality. In the presence of the Crucified, the hated unrighteousness seems to the soul like the crucifixion of his Lord, and the coveted righteousness takes on the form of affectionate desire to be joined to the personal Saviour.

This wondrous transformation of a man's moral sensibilities marks an epoch in his life. It is so novel and unexpected that he feels he never tried to produce it, he did not know how. It came to him from abroad and worked within him.

Something not himself has grasped his very self, and inspired him with the transcendent consciousness; and as he traces back the steps of that consciousness he marks the footprints, side by side with his own, of Christ's blessed Paraclete, the Holy Ghost, Lord of his moral life.

But there is yet one more step for the soul and one more work for the Holy Ghost before the gracious victory is complete. There must be the glad surrender of faith that shall bring the soul and Christ actually together. Thus far his conscience was touched and awakened by another. His affections and desires were separate from their old objects almost in spite of himself. The process of change was hardly a matter of consciousness, certainly not a matter of volition. He has been the passive recipient of influence, and to this point his active powers have been idle. These active powers are gathered and represented in his will. His true personality resides in it alone. It is the organ of his selfhood. Shall his will bear him on to the cross? It is the pivot question of his life of lives. Is the Holy Ghost the Sovereign Lord of his volition? Does God control the will? This is the great question of the ages, perhaps of the eternities. It is the first puzzling problem of human thought, and human thought never sees its way out of it.

Two parties of thinkers stand in opposite ranks, and can do nothing but flaunt their banners in each other's faces and claim the victory.

Liberty and necessity, God's sovereignty and Man's freedom,—the earliest philosophy took up the question, and the latest philosophy has not laid it down. If the Holy Ghost is lord of my will, how am I responsible? If my will is free, then how am I dependent on the Holy Ghost? The answer to this question must take the form of compromise, or at least must be content with demonstrating the facts and leaving the reconciling of them to rest among the mysteries. We may, for example, demonstrate the absolute sovereignty of God by arguments the most conclusive, without a flaw in the premises or a single hitch in the train of deduction, and having done so, we may sum up the conclusion, and label it "proved" and place it away on some shelf of the mind.

And then we may demonstrate the freedom of the human will by proof different from the other, but still conclusive,—by the testimony of consciousness, a basic proof, the ultimate source and foundation of all conviction. And this conclusion we may label "proved," and lay it on the shelves of the mind.

Thus we have the two statements, each one demonstrated as an infallible truth by the only evidence that is adapted to the case. Both are true; yet when we take down these shelved conclusions, and compare them with one another, they are mutually contradictory, and our reason cries out in despair for a light that God has not given. In this ignorance we must walk, content to know that somewhere in the hidden councils of the upper world the problem has a solution.

It is a remarkable fact in the study of this controversy that while man's speculative reason demurs at accepting this contradictory position of liberty and necessity, sovereignty and freedom, his experimental conviction embraces them both in one fervid belief that makes the very life and joy of his religion. When any soul, under the lead of the awakened conscience and the heavenly longing, inspired by the Holy Ghost, does actually surrender its will, with all its engrossment of heart and life, to the faith and service of Jesus Christ, the process seems to bear a twofold consciousness: on the one hand, there is the deepest laid sense that there never was an act of its life so profoundly and delightedly free as that act of self-surrender, and at the same moment there is a conviction, not less deep, that the freedom was not an independent freedom, that the will was not self-moved. And when the dedicated soul stands upon its feet again, full of the sense of its new, free, spiritual manhood, the first breath of its freedom will utter itself in the ascription, "Not unto me, not unto me, but unto Thee, O Holy Ghost, Sovereign Lord of my moral life!" Many speculative difficulties are solved by experiment; and as there is no difficulty so bewildering to the reason as this difficulty of man's freedom and dependence, so none ever had such an illustrious solution in the deepest experimental consciousness of the soul.

But although the current of our life passes thus between two rocky abutments, rising up in a perpendicular antagonism that no earthly theory can reconcile, yet we know that beyond the vapory height of our vision, in the bright depth of God's counsels, the separation is firmly bridged over, and the repugnant ideas are linked into structural unity of truth.

There is another agency of the Holy Ghost, as the agent and commissioner of Christ, which cannot be passed by,—his agency, namely, in giving efficacy to the appointed means of grace, the preaching and the sacraments of the church.

It is interesting to know, if we can, in what way a spiritual agency can work through material means. The word of God is the Sword of the Spirit, piercing even to the dividing asunder of soul and spirit. Does its Divine efficacy depend upon the sharpness of the instrument or on the susceptibility of the hearer and reader of the word?

Does the Holy Ghost cause the truths of salvation to be any more true at one time than at another, or does he work among the moral sensibilities of the heart to make an entrance for the truth? The word of God as a vehicle of the truth of God, is it not just as full of truth at one time as at another? Is there an ebb and flow of meaning in his revealed word? Is it not always full of himself? If it be the same revelation, then there can be no influence of the Holy Ghost upon the word, to make it more or less; but as God opened the heart of Lydia to receive the things that were spoken by Paul, so must it always be. We can conceive that he who is Lord of the soul's life can, by the affinity of nature, work among its motive powers, mellow its feelings, abate its self-conceit, exalt its ambitions, tone down its antagonisms, create a holy hunger and thirst, so that when the oft-rejected word of God comes to it again, it may find a heart already prepared and opened by the Holy Ghost.

Its efficacy, therefore, lies not in any new property imparted to the truth itself, but in the quickening of the soul, touched by the kindred life of the Divine Spirit.

And must we not say the same of the sacraments? Is the baptismal water imbued with a quality of the Holy Ghost, so that its bathing touch shall send a quickening shock to the soul of sin? Do the bread and wine take into themselves such a property of positive holiness, that they carry to the lips of every recipient the body and blood of the Crucified? Material substances may be charged with material forces, that communicate themselves to other material things. Heat and electricity and magnetism are diffusible properties, and spread themselves by fixed laws of material affinity, but a moral force gathered into a material substance is out of the analogy of things. A property of unintelligent matter communicating a force to the intelligent and moral soul is an idea that has no resembling fact in all the world. Why should we suppose such a diversity of method in the working of the Holy Ghost, now influencing the spirit of man by conviction, by persuasion, by comforting, by awakening, by inspiring, and all by a direct illapse,—the moral grasping the moral, the spiritual embracing the spiritual, in perfect and beautiful congruity; and then directing itself to produce the same spiritual results by outside unspiritual means,—material forces acting to stir that one thing with which in all the world material things are most out of harmony, the spirit and soul of man. The dispensation under which we live is the dispensation of the Spirit; and must not all his influence on us, and our reciprocal approaches towards him, be after the nature of spirit life and spirit communion? To suppose that a material, mechanical substance can be charged with the property of holiness seems to wipe out all the distinctions of thought, requires a revision of our dictionaries. Instead of that sublime exercise of faith in which the soul holds conscious converse with its unseen but not distant Lord, it substitutes a simple belief of the external fact that the Holy Ghost is mingled in with the matter of the sacrament. If the one be faith worthy of the noblest Christian manhood, the other would seem to be the inadequate conception of the child period of the spiritual life.

Let us rather believe thus, then: The Spirit bears witness with our spirits, spiritually and not materially, and though He makes a covenanted use of those Divine occasions when God's word is taught and his sacraments are administered, to quicken our affections, strengthen our faith, exalt our hopes, fortify our consciences, and to stamp our souls with the seal of his assurance, yet is he not fettered to occasions nor incorporated with material means; but with the glorious power of his omnipresence he besets us behind and before, about our path and about our bed, strengthens, comforts, upholds us, gives us grace to live as becomes us and to die in the peace of his felt communion. In a word, he takes the things of Christ and shows them to us, stands to us in Christ's place, as if he were Christ, making us to know all that we can know of Christ on earth, and then, as the Lord of our lives, presenting us, cleansed with his own unction, to the adorable Saviour, whom not having seen the Holy Ghost had taught us to love, and in him to rejoice with a joy unspeakable and full of glory. Then the vicegerent office of the Holy Ghost is fulfilled, though his sweetness abides with us forever in the communion of Father, Son, and Holy Ghost, with the redeemed, who shall die no more.

Studies in the History of the Prayer Book.

[The Anglican Reform. The Puritan Innovations. The Elizabethan Reaction. The Caroline Settlement.] With Appendices.

By HERBERT MORTIMER LUCKOCK, D.D., author of "After Death."

12mo, cloth, uncut edges, ... *Price, $1.50.*

"The Canon of Ely has already distinguished himself by his book, 'After Death.' In that publication he proved himself the possessor of a fine intellect and a well trained pen. In his new work, entitled 'Studies in the History of the Prayer Book,' he fully maintains the standard of his first treatise. His divisions have a ring about them very like the touch of that master of English history, John Richard Green. The reader feels that in following such a teacher he has at least a living thought as the clue to guide him among the intricacies and technicalities of liturgical study. Dr. Luckock does not seem to have reached the very highest round in the ladder of Anglican Catholicity, but is well up in that direction. He is near enough to Dean Stanley to emulate the realistic touches in 'The History of the Eastern Church,' and at the same time is near enough to Canon Liddon to preserve his clearness of statement on theological points. He has succeeded in clothing some very dry bones with flesh quite rosy and palpitating. The book is thoroughly polished and attractive, and must secure a decided success as the most readable work of its special class."—*The Episcopal Register.*

"It is just the book that every student of the Prayer Book has wanted."—*Standard of the Cross.*

"Liturgical development is becoming a matter of absorbing interest, not only within but without the Church, and the work of Canon Luckock may be regarded as a valuable contribution to the literature of the subject."—*The Churchman.*

Thomas Whittaker, Publisher, 2 & 3 Bible House, N. Y.

ANDREW JUKES' NEW WORK.

The New Man and the Eternal Life.

Notes on the Reiterated Amens of the Son of God. By ANDREW JUKES, author of "Types of Genesis," "The Restitution of all Things," "The Law of the Offerings," "Characteristic Differences of the Four Gospels," etc.

296 pp., 12mo, cloth, . . . Price, $1.75.

"'Verily, verily!' Many times did our Lord employ these introductory terms in His discourse. * * * At twelve distinct times does Christ arouse attention to specific doctrines of the kingdom by such reiterations. Our author takes up these twelve cases and develops the respective deliverances of the Saviour in the connection. He writes with intense feeling, and with a fullness of Scripture knowledge which seems exceptional. There is much that is stimulating and suggestive, both in the conception of his work and in its execution. * * * The work is a most helpful one, and makes a worthy addition to the list of books already published by this author."—*The Standard,* Chicago.

"Andrew Jukes is a voluminous writer, but he is an original and profound thinker as well. His 'New Man and the Eternal Life' is one of the most original and ingenious of his works, and will have, as it ought to have, a large circulation in this country."—*The Parish Visitor.*

"We have found the book suggestive and spiritually stimulating."—*The Congregationalist.*

"They who want a rich feast may herein eat and be satisfied. 'The New Man' should be read slowly and with concentration; thus every particle will be enjoyed."—*The Living Church.*

"The argument throughout the book is well sustained and intensely interesting. Entirely original, it is a book which will be read and re-read with ever-increasing pleasure and profit."—*The Church Guardian,* Halifax.

THOMAS WHITTAKER, Publisher,
2 & 3 BIBLE HOUSE, NEW YORK.

One volume, handsomely printed, 334 pp., 12mo, cloth extra, $1.50.

Modern Heroes of the Mission Field.

By the Rt. Rev. W. PAKENHAM WALSH, D.D., Bishop of Ossary, Ferns and Leighlin. Author of "Heroes of the Mission Field," "The Moabite Stone," etc.

CONTENTS:

I. Henry Martyn: India and Persia, 1805–1812.
II. William Carey: India, 1793–1834.
III. Adoniram Judson: Burmah, 1813–1850.
IV. Robert Morrison: China, 1807–1834.
V. Samuel Marsden: New Zealand, 1814–1838.
VI. John Williams: Polynesia, 1817–1839.
VII. William Johnson: West Africa, 1816–1823.
VIII. John Hunt: Fiji, 1838–1848.
IX. Allen Gardiner: South America, 1835–1851
X. Alexander Duff: India, 1829–1864.
XI. David Livingstone: Africa, 1840–1873.
XII. Bishop Patteson: Melanesia, 1855–1871.

"The American reading world owes a debt of thanks to the publisher for bringing out so good a book in a style of type and paper which leaves nothing to be desired. The book is one which must be read by those who would know its merits. No newspaper notice can do justice to it."—*The Living Church.*

"It is entitled to a place in every library, and should be purchased and read by every one interested in the work of Foreign Missions."—*Gospel in all Lands.*

"A good book to have in hand if one is to keep the divine spirit of the missionary work close to his heart."—*Standard of the Cross.*

THOMAS WHITTAKER, Publisher,
2 & 3 BIBLE HOUSE, NEW YORK.

Ecclesia Anglicana.

A History of the Church of Christ in England, from the Earliest to the Present Times. By ARTHUR CHARLES JENNINGS, M.A. With marginal Summaries of paragraphs, and full alphabetical Index.

502 pp., 12mo, cloth, red edges, . . . *Price, $2.25.*

"At last we have a book on the *whole* history of the Church of England that will be a boon to the professor of ecclesiastical history and a comfort to his students. Put together Bates' College Lectures, Carwithen, Churton, Short, and all the other books through which we used to be obliged to wade in order to acquaint ourselves, tolerably, with the history of our Church, and we should not do more than begin to approach to exact knowledge of its history which Mr. Jennings has furnished us in this single volume. * * * He follows none of the old style types of so-called history, which consists mainly in hero-building. Every man, no matter who, stands or fa'ls, by him, according to his personal worth and actual value in the Church events of his time. Altogether, this work is destined for long use by students of its subject, and we regard its production as one of the noticeable events of the present year."—*The Living Church.*

"An unusually good book."—*The Am. Literary Churchman.*

"One of the most needed and best written historical manuals which has appeared for a long time."—*The Standard of the Cross.*

"The volume is packed with information, given generally in a clear, vivid way."—*The Independent.*

"We know of no general history of the English Church which is as likely to be as serviceable as this, and we are glad to recommend it to our readers."—*The Churchman.*

THOMAS WHITTAKER, Publisher,
Nos. 2 & 3 BIBLE HOUSE, NEW YORK.

www.ingramcontent.com/pod-product-compliance
Lightning Source LLC
Chambersburg PA
CBHW020103170426
43199CB00009B/381